Heal and Forgive

This grab-you-in-the-gut first-hand account of growing up in an abusive household should be read by anyone who has ever wondered: Is what I experienced abusive? Is what I experienced as a child abusive? Is what I am permitting abusive? Or, Is what I am doing abusive?

Written with refreshing clarity, objectivity and frank matter-of factness, many readers will recognize themselves and be touched by Nancy's straightforward voice of validation. This author leads the reader deftly into the still largely uncharted controversial and confusing arena of forgiveness: What is it? When is it appropriate? How does it or doesn't it link with my healing? She offers wonderful signposts and resources along the way for the person wending their way through the wilderness of recovery from the silent inner pain abusive families inflict.

This is a powerful contribution to the field of recovery from abuse. I will recommend it to many of my clients.

Chris Richards, M.S.W.

Heal and Forgive is an eloquent examination of survival and ultimately, spiritual prosperity that holds promise for abuse survivors seeking the next level in healing and for anyone who wishes to further understand the tragedy of abuse.

Mark Hardy, Attorney

Heal and Forgive is a sensitive and perceptive book that would be very helpful for anyone who has been abused. This is a very personal odyssey of self-discovery, pain, revelations, discouragement, hope, healing and forgiving. The author offers perceptive and knowledgeable insights and reveals much about the difficult and often baffling process of healing that can occur as a result of facing abuse. This helpful and compassionate book is a blueprint for surviving the pain of abuse and reconstructing a healthy life.

Judy M. Harris, M.A.,
Licensed Marriage and Family Therapist

Heal and Forgive is compelling, essential reading for the adult survivor of childhood abuse. Like the author, I also found forgiveness to be fleeting, difficult and unfulfilling. Ms. Richards, through her life experiences has been able to lay out a concise blueprint that will promote personal healing. I now have renewed faith that forgiveness, inner-peace and happiness are truly possible.

Daryl Frank, Adult Survivor

Powerful ... compelling ... *Heal and Forgive* clearly outlines the steps necessary to forgive an abuser. This is an excellent read for anyone looking for direction with his or her own recovery from abuse or with the struggle to forgive.

Janice Selander

Heal and Forgive

Forgiveness
in the
Face of Abuse

NANCY RICHARDS

with a Foreword
by
MARIE M. FORTUNE

Blue Dolphin Publishing

Published by Blue Dolphin Publishing, Inc.
P.O. Box 8, Nevada City, CA 95959
Orders: 1-800-643-0765
Web: www.bluedolphinpublishing.com

ISBN: 1-57733-158-3

Library of Congress Cataloging-in-Publication Data

Richards, Nancy, 1957-
  Heal and forgive : forgiveness in the face of abuse / Nancy
Richards, with a foreword by Marie M. Fortune.
      p. cm.
  Includes bibliographical references.
  ISBN 1-57733-158-3 (pbk. : alk. paper)
  1. Richards, Nancy, 1957- 2. Child abuse—United States—
Case studies. 3. Victims of family violence—United States—
Case studies. 4. Adult child abuse victims—United States—
Case studies. 5. Forgiveness. I. Fortune, Marie M. II. Title.

HV6626.52.R53 2005
616.85'82239—dc22

                                                    2005008355

Printed in the United States of America

5   4   3   2   1

In order to forgive, we must experience healing.
When we forgive, we experience love.

Contents

Foreword

This story is painful to read. How can a parent abuse or allow the other parent to abuse children in the myriad of ways described here? Perhaps this "why?" has no answer. An answer would be helpful because part of what we humans long for in the midst of pain and chaos is to make some sense of it all. Answering "why?" there is such suffering in the world at least gives us a handle on it. Yet these answers are hard to come by. Suffering is a part of life. So is joy. But this is little solace to a child whose world is constructed by abuse.

Richards tells her story and unravels the process of healing that can lead to forgiveness. Along the way she breaks the silence of her family and is determined to tell the truth about her childhood. In spite of the denial by other family members, she is heard, believed and acknowledged by others in her life. She goes through the anger and grief of coming to terms with her childhood. She resists the temptation to "forgive and forget" because she knows it would only heal the wound lightly, saying "peace, peace," when there is no peace (Jeremiah 6:14). She puts her energy into protecting and caring for herself and in raising her children in a healthy, nurturing environment. All of this contributes to her healing; all of this is part of experiencing justice. All of this is what finally frees her to forgive and get on with her life.

She chose the path of healing and it took her to forgiveness. Forgiveness is not an obligation on the part of someone who has been harmed. It is not a solo act but rather takes place in community where we can find some sense of justice. It is not saying magic words and hoping that healing will come from that. It is hard work for the individual. It is God's grace carrying us the whole way. It is possible but never easy. This story is a testament to the possibility of healing and forgiveness. No cheap grace here. No pretense of keeping family secrets and denial. Just hard work and a great reward.

Rev. Marie M. Fortune
FaithTrust Institute, Seattle

Preface

Have you ever heard a remarkable story of forgiveness and wondered how the "victim" forgave? I have. People struggle with forgiveness every day. Sometimes we witness someone struggling over a seemingly trivial hurt and it is hard for us to fathom why the "injured" party can't forgive. Other times, people wrestle with injuries so monumental that to forgive seems like nothing less than mental defect.

For survivors of childhood abuse, forgiveness is particularly daunting. Many survivors of childhood trauma ask, "How do you forgive someone who has never asked to be forgiven; somebody who has never even acknowledged any wrongdoing, someone who continues to do the same thing? How do you forgive an offender and still protect yourself from re-injury?"

Heal and Forgive: Forgiveness in the Face of Abuse is a description not only of abuse, but also of denial.

Terrifying reports of child abuse are in the news every day. Many accounts are so horrific it is difficult to believe any adult is capable of treating a helpless child so callously. Our natural tendency is to deny the truth, protect our illusions, and avoid unpleasantness.

Before the abused can even consider forgiveness—they must be heard!

Forgiveness is a powerful expression of love. The question is—How do we express love in the face of abuse?

Deciding whether to forgive my abusers was a spiritual question for me; the choice to forgive was a spiritual commitment. However, in order to achieve forgiveness we must first perform the necessary psychological work.

We have all heard, "You must forgive in order to heal." It is my experience that you must heal in order to forgive.

Healing begins with the validation of our experiences.

Our greatest opportunity for healing comes from the offender. When the person who harmed us is willing to offer restitution, we are truly blessed. This means the offender must be willing to acknowledge the harm they caused us, offer a genuine apology, demonstrate a willingness to restore what was taken and change their abusive behavior. However, if the offender is not willing to acknowledge or stop the abuse, healing is still available to us.

First, we need to step outside the abusive family system to receive validation and acknowledgment from other sources. Second, we need to find appropriate ways to express our anger, to mourn, and to protect others and ourselves. Only then can we consider forgiveness.

This is a first-hand account of child abuse; a story of denial, a testimonial of healing, and ultimately a documentation of forgiveness.

I'll tell you my story as it happened.

Acknowledgments

I would like to express my thanks to my children, Tara and Dawn Melanson, and my life-partner, Bill Petschl, for their constant love and support. I love you with all my heart and I am forever grateful to share our caring family. I thank Paul Clemens, publisher of Blue Dolphin Publishing, Inc., for his belief in my message and for sharing that message with others. Thanks also to Ursula Bacon for her contribution to this work.

CHAPTER ONE

Father, Where Are You?

*Sometimes you just have to take the leap,
and build your wings on the way down.*
—Kobi Yamada

I remember quite a bit about my early childhood. I had all the love in the world to grow on. My parents provided all the fun that goes with a happy childhood and the warmth and closeness that makes family life secure and content. I loved my father and my mother. My parents had married very young: Mom was only seventeen and Dad barely twenty-one years old. I had "young" parents. My brother Rob was the firstborn; I arrived seventeen months later. Randy didn't appear on the scene for another five years. Dad cared deeply for his family and was a great and affectionate father. Mom was devoted to him, had fun with us kids, and took good care of our growing family.

We were a happy, contented family. My father, a gentle, loving man with a great sense of humor, was well-liked by friends, family members and his co-workers. He was a successful aeronautics engineer, and several of his ideas were used in various space programs.

1

Mom kept house, loved being a hostess, and entertained Dad's business associates and their friends regularly. She was also involved in many of our childhood activities. She was talented in many things, but especially liked to paint in oil. She created some lovely pieces that graced our home. We lived in a beautiful, spacious house in a fine Seattle neighborhood, and spent many weekends and summer vacations at our country cabin on Lake Roesiger. We learned to water ski, explored the woods, and romped through countless carefree days at the lake. Family members and friends were steady weekend visitors—all of whom Mom and Dad entertained royally.

Life was good. I felt safe and loved. But tragically, life changed.

When I was nine years old, my beloved father died unexpectedly of a brain aneurysm. He died at the age of thirty-three. With his passing, it seemed the sun stopped shining on our family. Mom sat for hours just staring into space with vacant eyes. She rarely ate anything and consequently lost thirty pounds.

I still remember those sad, sad days. I took the loss of my father very hard, and was inconsolable for a long time. Part of my world was gone, nothing was right and nothing was whole.

Fortunately, Dad left us well provided for, and Mom was able to maintain our comfortable lifestyle. However, she was at a loss about business matters. She had left everything to Dad and never had to cope on her own.

Shortly after my father's death, a draftsman and former co-worker of his started to drop in on Mom, offering to help her pick up the pieces. Ed had been a frequent visitor at our cabin at the lake, where we spent many summer weekends and holidays. He always stood out from the other guests because of the attention he lavished on us kids. He played with us, teased us, and was an all-around great guy. Somehow, he had appointed himself Mom's advisor and companion, as well as playing big-buddy of us kids. We liked the handsome, friendly man. He was fun!

Ten short months later, Mom married Ed. I was thrilled to see her happy again and was glad to have a "father" once more. No different than my mother, I felt vulnerable and frightened without Dad at our side. Now, with a husband at mother's side and a new "dad" for us kids, I could see our family come together again.

My brothers and I eagerly awaited their return from the honeymoon. The day after Mom and Ed returned my world of renewed vigor and expectations came crashing down. Life would never, never be the same again. If the loss of my father had caused me countless hours of pain and despair, the new regime Ed brought to the house would make past hurts seem insignificant.

Decades later, in therapy, I was finally able to label this man my mother had married. Mom's new husband was not only physically and emotionally abusive, but he was afflicted with Sadistic Behavior Disorder.

Many parents have abused their children to varying degrees. Most parents, however, dispense abusive punishment unintentionally and unaware. A person with Sadistic Behavior Disorder dispenses his or her abuse with cold, calculated intention and pleasure.

Although the concept was confusing and unbelievable at first, it took us little time to recognize that Ed actually liked to see us in pain. The first morning as a new family was quite memorable. Mom had warned us the night before that, contrary to the old ways with our father, the master bedroom would be off limits to us. There would be no running in and out, no morning greeting or playing games. Saturday morning, my brothers and I played peacefully in Rob's bedroom, anxiously waiting for Mom and Ed to wake up and start our exciting new life together.

Suddenly, the door of the master bedroom flew open! Ed moved quickly down the hall while our grim-faced mother appeared in Rob's doorway. She told us that Ed was very angry with us for making too much noise. We had neither been fighting nor yelling and protested against being called "noisy."

Just then Ed appeared in the doorway to Rob's room holding a wooden paddle from one of our games in his hand. With face muscles tight, he turned to my youngest brother.

"Randy," he directed sharply, "grab your ankles."

To my amazement and horror, just as my five-year-old brother's little hands clenched tightly around his ankles, a tremendous crack broke the uncomfortable hush that lingered in the room. Randy jumped into the air, clutched his buttocks, and ran to his room, screaming in pain and surprise.

Undisturbed, Ed commanded Rob to grab his ankles in a harsh voice.

As if hypnotized into submission, my eleven-year-old brother complied. Ed swung his arm back, and another loud crack resounded through the air. He hit Rob with such force that the paddle broke, flew across the room, crashed into the wall, and clattered noisily to the floor. Rob's face turned red. He averted his eyes as he fled to his bed.

Without missing a beat, Ed turned to me, and said in a voice void of emotions, "I am very angry I have to use my hand on you. It isn't fair for me to hurt my hand because you are a bad child. Grab your ankles, Nancy."

He hit my ten-year-old frame so hard I barely kept from losing my balance and crashing on my face. I ran to my room in tears. My bottom was on fire. My mind raced to figure out just what happened—so quickly and so violently. What had we done? Why this kind of cruel punishment? For what? What could I do to prevent this from happening again?

In the safety of my room, I hovered gingerly on the edge of my bed, my buttocks stinging from the blow. I thought about what had just happened. In my short ten years, never had I heard anybody talk about anything like this. Little did I know at the time, this incident would pale in comparison with what the future held for me.

Later in the day, I approached my mother hoping to find solace. Mom told me that Ed found us ill behaved— "the worst kids he had ever seen."

"Nobody else has ever told us that we are terrible children," I challenged my mother in a hurt and passionate voice.

Mom looked at me crossly and said, "Ed said that your father spoiled you and you have terrible manners. He said he is going to whip you into shape. And," she added firmly, "I am grateful for his help."

I was very confused.

In the meantime, Ed was in the garage busily building a new paddle. When he finished with his handiwork, the paddle was eighteen inches long, about six inches wide, and close to one inch thick. It was an awesome-looking thing and promised to pack a hefty wallop. Ed found a special spot in the kitchen to keep his weapon "handy." Our new stepfather showed "It" off with glee to visitors while a broad smile played across his face. No one commented on the damage such an instrument of punishment could inflict. Instead, the visitor usually produced a weak grin of his own.

As a young child, I interpreted each visitor's silence as approval of Ed's behavior and disapproval of my own. It wasn't until I was an adult that people expressed to me that even when they did not approve of another parent's methods, they were uncomfortable interfering in someone else's "family business." This was the conventional wisdom of the day.

No matter how hard we tried to stay out of his way, Ed found or invented almost daily transgressions of his rules that would warrant the use of severe punishment. After a while, all he had to do was look at one of us and issue a curt "Grab 'em!" and our young and slender backs would bend round, slim arms reached down in haste to grasp bony ankles, anticipating the painful and cruel moment when the hard, heavy piece of wood would connect forcefully with a tender backside.

Mom watched in silent acquiescence. She was of the old school that taught women to step back and fiercely guard the illusion of family unity at any cost. She was a graduate of the same school that instructed women that they are nothing without a man, and that solely through the acquisition of a male partner do women validate their existence. Independence of thought and action was recommended only as long as it blended with that of their mates.

After the loss of Dad, Mom immediately sought to shelter her insecurities and fears under the mantle of remarriage—a man to run her business affairs, a man to take over, to take control of what she considered her runaway life. This came first.

One day my sweet and innocent five-year-old brother Randy—whom the neighbors called "Rosy" because of his red hair and cherub-like disposition—had for some unknown reason elicited Ed's anger.

The harsh command, "Grab 'em, Randy" thundered through the kitchen, and I watched with horror as the blow cracked across my little brother's small behind. Randy jumped, screamed with pain, and grabbed his burning buttocks.

Ed turned on him with renewed fury, and informed him he had just broken the new rule of letting go of his ankles without permission.

"Just for that," Ed screamed in undisguised rage, "you'll get two more," and with that hauled off with the heavy wooden paddle, hitting him again. Little Randy flew across the kitchen and landed face first on the cold linoleum floor in a dark corner of the room, crying but still holding onto his ankles. Ed grabbed my terrified brother around the waist, set him upright, and administered the second blow.

I stood trance-like without moving a muscle, unable to help, powerless to prevent the next beating. I imagined myself safe in my room, away from the scene of the pain. That was the moment I laid the groundwork for disassociating myself from the events around me, learning to put myself in a trance and shut off my feelings. This then became my tactics for survival.

The clinical definition of disassociation is a distur-
bance or alteration in the normally integrative functions of
identity, memory, or consciousness. In children this may
occur following physical abuse or trauma. For me, it took
decades to recognize this behavior.

But my turn of "Grab 'em" came a short time later
when Ed inspected a spotless kitchen that I, with the help
of Randy, had cleaned up after dinner. Everything
sparkled, everything was neat and in perfect order, everything was in its place. Ed was a thorough inspector, looking
for anything he could apply to breaking the rules—nebu-
lous as they were. To his question if I had done a good job,
I replied with a proud "Yes."

Regardless of the impeccable appearance of the
kitchen, Ed's search for flaws was relentless. His eyes
roamed the sink and the counters with forensic accuracy.
His search was rewarded. Finally he discovered some cof-
fee ground residue adhered to the dish towel.

With his face dark and stormy and his voice grim and
threatening, he turned to me. "You lied to me. You didn't
do a good job. Grab 'em!" Helpless, unable to run, I bent
over, grabbed my ankles, and the painful whack of the hard
wooden paddle crashed down on my bottom.

Sitting down on my bruised behind after what became
the painful results of the routine beatings was more than
painful, but the emotional impact of the blows far exceeded
the physical pain. Long after our tender bottoms healed,
our hurt feelings continued to bleed, turning to acid,
corroding and corrupting our hearts and souls.

Only once did I witness Ed perpetrate any form of
violence against my mother. It happened at the dinner

table one evening. Ed in a moment of fury, knocked Mom forcefully out of her chair and onto the floor. My mother broke her fall by extending her arms behind her. She yelled vehemently from her unexpected spot on the kitchen linoleum, "Do that again and we're done!"

Ed never hurt my mother again. It was clear to me and I'm sure to Ed, that Mom would not tolerate his mistreatment of her.

All through the next six years, Ed's military regime never let up and continued to worsen. With a white handkerchief wrapped around his finger, Ed would relentlessly check the most obscure places for dust.

Although we kept our rooms according to the enlisted men's journal of procedure—with socks rolled just so, underwear folded a certain way, shirts and sweaters in a meticulous row, all hangers in the closet pointing in the same direction, and every spot in our rooms at inspection status, we never passed weekly inspection and were punished accordingly. There was no end to his creativity when it came to cruel punishment. He found great satisfaction in creating terror and havoc among us. I would suddenly hear the sounds of furniture being forcefully tossed and scattered noisily, which was followed by Ed's heavy footsteps pounding the floor in our direction, appearing on the scene, selecting one of us at random, and beating us up for an imaginary infraction of his latest rule.

From another part of the house, he could hear the sound of a glass of milk spilling on the floor and like shot from a cannon, he appeared on the scene of the accident in a flash. Rob was bending over, rag in hand, about to mop up the telltale signs of his spill, when Ed reached down, pushed Rob's face toward the floor, and moved his head back and around, roughly rubbing his nose in the spill—just like a dog.

Most families use the dinner hour as a time to get together—to talk about the events of the day, acknowledge each other, make plans, and in general, be together. That was not the case in our household. Dinner was a scheduled nightmare giving Ed the unopposed opportunity to come up with surprise acts of cruelty.

The dinner table was our parade ground to strut our best table manners, which were impeccable: we kept our free hand on our laps along with the napkin; we chewed with our mouths shut; our elbows never touched the table; we always said please and thank you. Knife blades were turned in properly at the top of the plate. We set the table with the precision of a drill team: napkins folded and placed just so, stemware sat at proper angles. Everything was picture-perfect.

Nothing was ever enough. Nothing right was ever right, nothing was ever perfect. There was not one meal when one of us wasn't routinely terrorized or abused. With unerring regularity, Ed would jab a fork into one of our tender arms or the backs of our hands. On many occasions, with fists doubled up, he knocked us off our chairs. Overtaken by surprise, our seats tipped back and mercilessly tossed us onto the hard kitchen floor.

When Randy once carelessly rested his elbow on the table for a brief moment, Ed in a deadly quiet voice, turned to him: "Randy, take your fork into your right hand; raise your left arm in the air, and jab yourself in your forearm with the fork as hard as you can. If you don't do it hard enough," Ed added, "I'll do it for you."

Randy, afraid of being jabbed by Ed, his usually rosy face white as a sheet, with a tortured grimace, clenched his eyes shut and jabbed himself as hard as he could. Screaming "Ouch! Ouch! Ouch!"—he broke the skin. Rob and I watched in horror. Mom didn't say a word.

Day after day I sat through the evening meal wrapped in terror, trying to stay out of harm's way. It didn't always work. There was the time when I extended my hands over my plate, in a gesture of pleading, not to be served the spinach Mom was dishing out. I hated spinach.

Ed grabbed the pan out of Mom's hands, and quick as the wind dumped a generous portion of the boiling-hot spinach on my hands. I cried out in agony as I peeled the offending greens from my hands, watching angry blisters form.

With nasty blisters on the back of my hands and a searing pain inside, I looked for help and comfort from my mother. She offered none. "You shouldn't have covered your plate with your hands," was her indifferent reply.

When my mother refused to help me, I turned to others for aid. There was neither understanding nor encouragement whenever I tried to talk to outsiders of what went on at home. On the contrary: "You should obey your stepfather.... You should try to understand your mother.... How can you be so selfish? Look at all you have."

Puzzled and shocked, I whirled in a vicious circle: If I never told, the abuse would never stop. If I did tell, insult was added to injury when my chosen confidant supported Mom and Ed.

As children, our young brains have not developed enough to take care of ourselves. We are dependent on the adults in our lives to teach us how to process the information we gather from our experiences. I learned as an adult that when our childhood abuse is denied as if it did not happen, or as if the violent behavior is excusable, our trauma becomes fused to us and stays with us until someone teaches us differently by validating our experiences. If our experiences are never validated, our trauma remains fused, even into adulthood.

There was no peaceful moment to be had when Ed was around. Fear stalked our hearts and souls, impending doom loomed permanently behind a door, in a corner of a room, and in our minds. It was the only sure thing we could rely on.

With all its pretty furnishing, the collection of gleaming silver and sparkling crystal pieces, the impeccable cleanliness and order of the household, the house was not a pleasant place to live. The walls echoed the cruel words that raked over us every day, and a layer of deep, dark anger laced the air. The occasional bursts of laughter were not the happy sounds of the fun games of children at play, but were the nervous response to the sadistic acts which Ed considered funny and insisted that we join in his distorted sense of merriment.

In a less than playful mood, Ed would pick on one of us kids and encourage the two bystanders to laugh at the discomfort of the unfortunate victim of the moment. Our laughter was the signal of approval for his cruel behavior. We simply did what was expected of us as a means of self-protection. It took the pressure off us for the time being. Our turn to be on the wrong end of the next sick joke was only a few moments away.

Our stepfather's sadistic sense of humor began to rub off on Rob and me. We often ganged up and teased young

Randy until he cried in anguish. At other times, Rob would trap me in one of his hurtful, unkind schemes that left me embarrassed and devastated. Every once in a while I would get even with him by pulling one of my stunts—keeping turmoil and discord alive.

It was not a normal kind of sibling bickering and getting each other into trouble with innocent and childish acts. We copied our role model until we truly hurt each other. It wasn't enough that we suffered from Ed's abuse; we tried his methods out on each other—after all, that's all we knew.

In response to our abuse, each of us began to take on a role. These roles were significant, because they defined how we coped not only as children, but how we later viewed our abuse as adults. I was the troublemaker when I fought against the abuse of my brothers and myself. Randy's role was to become the invisible one, while Rob proclaimed himself Mom's protector by not complaining about Ed's acts, and insisted Randy and I do the same.

These coping mechanisms were well rooted in us by the time I was in the sixth grade, and Ed introduced the ultimate game at the dinner table. Prior to the evening meal, we were playing a game on the living room floor. Whenever we were called to the table, we had learned to drop what we were doing and rush at top speed to our places at the table.

When the call to dinner came one particular evening, we were in a quandary. If we cleaned up the game and packed it away, our arrival at the table would be delayed— an unpardonable infraction punishable by a beating. If we didn't pick up the game and simply rushed to the table, we would be severely punished for not being orderly.

What to do?

We chose to rush to the table. There was no right in our lives; there was only wrong. Right became wrong, and nothing escaped Ed's eager eye. He glommed on to every opportunity or better yet, created one. He glanced at the living room and saw the game board in the middle of the floor. Sure as rain, Ed had his case for the evening.

"You're slobs! I'm furious with you slobs. You didn't pick up your game. Careless, thoughtless slobs! I'll teach you a lesson. We'll play a new game you won't forget."

"Rob, Randy, Nancy," he continued a sadistic grin across his hard mouth, "you will form a circle in the living room. You'll all grab your ankles, and I'll hand Rob the paddle. Rob will hit Nancy as hard as he can." He looked piercingly at my brother.

"Rob," he continued, "if you don't hit Nancy hard enough, she gets the paddle and hits you as hard as she can. Then she'll turn to Randy and hit him as hard as she can. If you do hit each other hard enough, you keep passing on the paddle, and so on," he concluded his instructions with a vague motion of his hand.

"I will referee the game and make sure you're playing it right," he added smugly.

I started to shake all over as I listened to Ed explain what he referred to as the "Paddle Game." My breath was labored, and I was so terrified I couldn't control the tremor that spread over my limbs. How does he think up these games? He and his games are straight from hell, I thought wildly. I had recognized the sadistic pleasure he derived from tormenting the boys and me.

Enough! I had enough. It was one thing for Ed to beat us, but I wouldn't be a part of beating my brothers. I looked around the table. Mom had "left town." Ed appeared highly pleased with himself, and the boys looked frightened and, at the same time, compliant.

I stood up, "I won't play," I stated shakily. Then I burst into tears and fled to my room.

Mom appeared in my room after a while, and in a sort of matter-of-fact voice tried to assure me that she would have stepped in and not permitted Ed to conduct the paddle game. I didn't believe her. For the past two years Mom had not stopped anything this man had done to us.

Before she left my room, Mom informed me she had decided to divorce Ed.

I felt both elated and worried at the same time. After all, for two years we had heard how much Mom and Ed cared for one another. We had also been told in no uncertain terms, that we were awful kids and were to blame for all the trouble the family endured. I was petrified that it would be my fault Mom's marriage ended in divorce.

Terrified of the consequences Mom's decision would have on me, and the load too heavy for my twelve-year-old psyche, I blurted out, "Mom, I know it is all my fault." Tears brimmed over in my eyes as I said, "I know that you and Ed would be happy together if it weren't for the problems the boys and I cause. I'm so sorry! I don't want you to be unhappy."

Mom readily agreed, "True! All we ever argue about is you kids. I love Ed," she said.

Devastated at the enormity of my obvious shortcomings and my responsibility for my mother's happiness, I said, "Okay, Mom, I'll play the paddle game."

"It's too late, Nancy," Mom frowned. Ed is packing his things. But you can go and ask him to stay."

For the sake of Mom's marriage and to rid myself of the responsibility for this mess, I trudged off to find Ed, who was in the master bedroom packing.

The tall man, who was unhurriedly stuffing things from a chest of drawers into a suitcase, stopped and straightened up when I entered the room. Without a preamble, without Hi or Hello, tears streaming down my face, I ran up to him, hugged the man I so desperately despised, and in a voice choked with emotion, I begged him to stay.

Ed, not wanting to appear too eager, grudgingly gave in to my pleas. Yes, he would stay, he grouchily acquiesced. I untangled my arms from reaching around him and left the room, numb and empty. I felt like a balloon with the air gone out, hovering aimlessly at low, so very low.

I now was the designated driver to steer the family's vehicle of all-around contentment on a safe course. I would have to stand up and try to prevent abuse, and take the blame if it didn't work. What a spot to be in. I felt little else but raw panic.

Rob raged at me mercilessly. "We could have been rid of the son-of-a bitch," he said hoarsely in the quiet of his room as he faced me. "You prevented that. What happens now will be your fault." He was furious.

From then on, Rob blamed me for every temper tantrum Ed displayed, every beating, every battering and the torrents of foul and nasty words directed at us.

As a child, I accepted Mom and Rob's blame. It was not until I was an adult that I realized that only Mom had the power to decide whether or not she would remain married to Ed. Mom handed the power and responsibility of her marital status and the protection of her family over to a twelve-year-old child incapable of adult thoughts and actions.

Rob beat me regularly as I tried desperately to get him to see it wasn't my fault. He wouldn't hear it. Now there were two people beating me and my circle of fear grew larger.

"We could have been rid of him," Rob hissed at me again and again. Wracked with guilt, I kept praying to God, asking Him to let me know that it wasn't my fault. If God indeed replied, I couldn't hear Him over the roar of my internal misery.

To understand is to forgive, even oneself.
—Alexander Chase

CHAPTER TWO

Continued
Reign of Terror

The mind does strange and tricky things to protect us. The older I got, the less my mind permitted me to experience my feelings as Ed relentlessly continued his reign of terror. He never let up. Like a bloodhound, he was forever on the trail of pursuit, sniffing out the most infinitesimal clues that might lead to the discovery of what he deemed "inappropriate behavior for the day."

One lazy Saturday afternoon, Ed picked up one of my skis and discovered a misplaced strap. He went into a burning fit of rage. Grabbing my skis like a baseball bat, he swung back and delivered a well-planned, powerful blow to my upper arm.

I clutched my throbbing limb and quickly fled the scene to report the incident to my mother. Ed ran after me howling objections and calling me a liar. When I pointed to the burning, angry, red bruise which began to blossom on my arm, Ed insisted shrilly to my mother that the injury had been caused by the skis falling on me.

Mom pulled me aside harshly. "Why do I always have this trouble with you; only you—never the boys?" she hissed. "Stop trying to make trouble and learn to get along."

Growing up became harder and harder for me without the support of my mother. Whenever I attempted to stand up for what was right, she slapped me down again. Each time I retreated into silent hopelessness and licked my wounds until I recovered sufficiently to stand up for myself again.

We did see a family therapist for a short period of time. Silently, we sneaked in and out of the counselor's office, hoping our visits would go unnoticed by friends and neighbors. Our new counselor was a sweet-natured, older person who at first appeared pleasant and capable of handling our problems. But my visits with her quickly became as frustrating as the rest of my life. As the woman listened to my tale of unbridled family violence, she nodded her head in knowing empathy, while the soft clicking of her knitting needles increased their speed in accordance with the rise and fall of my voice.

Every once in a while the counselor would utter a complacent uh, uh, uh-ha, and occasionally break in with an irritating "Okay, ducky, okay"—an aggravating vestige of her Australian background.

This therapist, who in session had listened to Ed's admission of severely beating us kids, advised me calmly to "just stay out of Ed's way."

When I told her Rob was beating me too, she replied, "Do nothing to anger them. If Ed or Rob yells at you or hits you, just say to yourself, 'This is not my problem'—and walk away."

When I challenged the "professional" advice heatedly, the counselor's appraisal of the situation did not change an iota. Again and again she recommended that, in spite of the difficult task, I was to turn the other cheek and walk away from my offenders. Undaunted by the facts which had come to light that ANYTHING and EVERYTHING made Ed and Rob mad, she repeated her recommendations.

"Follow my advice," she insisted. "It will work. I am the expert here," she reminded me, barely raising her eyes from her knitting. My burden weighed heavier and heavier, until I thought I would be crushed by the sheer weight of it.

Counseling sessions stopped and we all carried on as "normal."

Until just recently, I did not realize that Washington State had laws in 1970 requiring professionals to report cases of abuse. According to the U.S. Department of Health and Human Services (http://www.acf.hhs.gov/programs/cb/laws/capta03/index.htm), in order for states to qualify for funding under the Child Abuse Prevention and Treatment Act (CAPTA), they must pass some form of a mandatory child abuse and neglect reporting law. CAPTA was originally passed in 1974. According to the Washington State Legislature (http://search.leg.wa.gov/pub/textsearch/ViewRoot.asp?Action=Html&Item=0&X=902101014&p=1), the state of Washington enacted RCW 26.44, commonly referred to as the Child Abuse and Neglect Reporting Act in 1965.

Our family therapist's failure to report the abuse left us unprotected and further instilled within me a feeling of responsibility for my own beatings.

Safety eluded me. In no way did I feel nurtured or comforted. I didn't believe I held a spot in anyone's heart—except Randy's. However, he was so little—I felt like it was my responsibility to nurture him—not his responsibility to nurture me.

One evening, when Randy was about eight years old, he quietly sneaked into my room. He sat next to me on the edge of my bed and thought for a moment before he spoke slowly. "Have you ever noticed, Nance, that sometimes Ed takes turns being extra mean to one of us for a couple of weeks? When it's our turn, there is nothing we can do to keep him from hurting us—and then he moves on and gives someone else a turn for a while?"

I looked at the pain and insight in Randy's young eyes and said softly, "Yes, I've noticed."

He wept quietly as he said, "It's my turn right now."

My eyes weld up with tears, "I know."

Randy crawled into my arms and cried, "Why is this happening, Nance?"

"I don't know."

Silently, with tears brimming in my eyes, I held my little brother close—rocking and crying, without saying a word. The silent moment of shared misery lasted a long time. Finally, Randy freed himself from my loving embrace and tiptoed quietly to his own room. I felt so helpless. I could suppress my own pain, but I could not suppress Randy's. Oh, how I wished it were my turn.

As children, we are unaware of our tactics for survival. We simply do whatever we can to go on.

I used many survival tactics as a child. Some methods I am aware of today—other methods I am certain continue to elude me. What I am sure of is that the very mechanisms that save us as children, harm us as adults.

I escaped reality in many different fashions. At night, in the quiet of my room, I dreamt of my father and of safety. Sometimes, I dreamed he would come back and rescue us.

When I was away from home, I was the "life of the party"—having extraordinary amounts of fun, while keeping the pain at bay.

I spent much of my home life unknowingly walking around in a self-induced trance, banishing my emotional self to a faraway, unreachable place. Other times at home, such as with Randy, I simply stepped in as the family mother.

* * * * *

At age fifteen, with my hands over my ears as if to drown out the ugliness of my stepfather's abuse, I sat by myself in the kitchen of my home. I had just been through one of Ed's standard tirades that had chipped away at the meager vestiges of self-worth that had survived the five years of his tyrannical regime.

This time the dinner table had not been completely set by the time Ed arrived home from work. It didn't matter that dinner was more than an hour away and we were almost done with the chore. This insignificant incident was enough fuel to fire up his rage and let go with a full-blown, screaming tirade. Another factor added to his fury. Both Rob and I were getting older and Ed was sensing the rising of a silent rebellion forming in us.

With paranoia in full bloom, Ed felt threatened by us. He was generally prone to believe that the world was out to get him. Paranoia, combined with his sadistic behavior patterns, left no room for reasoning with him.

"You're all slobs. Worthless slobs, no-good brats who don't deserve a home like this," he thundered on for starters as we shrank within ourselves. Going inside was the only place left to hide. But hiding from the attack ended quickly for me when he brutally pulled me by my hair, yanking my head up.

"Look at me when I'm talking to you, damn you. You're going to learn, you slob!" he roared at me.

The features of Ed's handsome face turned into a contorted grimace of cold and calculated fury and left no room for the slightest hint of kindness. A thick vein stood out on his forehead and his hand curled into a fist, ready to strike at will. Rob and Randy sat at rigid attention through the ordeal, eyes fixed dutifully on Ed's face.

A hot and searing anger rushed up all the way into my throat and held fast in every inch of my being. Disregarding the pain, I whipped my head around pulling my hair loose from his grip. "Sit down!" he said.

I looked at this despicable man whose abuse I had endured for five years: "I'm not going to sit down again. I'm not going to be hurt again—ever," I said, a note of fierce independence ringing in my voice.

My attempt to leave the room was stunted immediately by my stepfather's stinging command: "You sit back down, or I'll sit you down so hard, you'll never get up again."

I looked at my mother beseechingly. Mom clasped her hands in prayer and motioned her head in the direction of my chair, beckoning me to sit down. I capitulated to my mother's silent request and sat down. I acquiesced in mute despair, my defiance put on hold. Ed had hurt me, but my mother had killed my spirit. The endless beatings and batterings were hard enough to endure, but my mother's attitude was unbearable—the betrayal incomprehensible.

"My God," my unspoken words roared bitterly in the silence of my mind, "why won't she help me?"

The next day, I withdrew into total silence. For two days I refused to speak and responded to my mother's attempts to converse with the same silence with which Mom witnessed Ed's treatment of us kids. Now the house was quiet; Mom had left on her errands, furious with my behavior. Ed was at work, and Rob and Randy were not around.

I was angry. I felt spent and helpless. I had no support from Mom, no resource, nothing. As welcome as the silence of the house may have been at the moment, the rooms remained strangely charged with the sound of fury and the ugly demeaning words the man had left behind. They flashed on and off in my mind's eye like a broken neon sign on a dark night.

I shook myself awake into the present, reached into my pant pocket, and pulled out a small, rumpled bit of paper. I smoothed out the yellow slip on which I had written a phone number. It was the number of a teen hotline posted on a bulletin board in school.

Determined, I grasped the telephone receiver tightly in my hand and dialed the number. The pleasant voice of a hotline volunteer answered the call, and patiently listened to my tale of pain and terror. To my question if Ed was a fit parent (this was the early seventies and I hadn't heard the term child-abuse), the woman replied crisply, "Absolutely not; not even close." She added without hesitation, "Your mother is not a fit parent either. She has a responsibility to not allow this to happen."

I was stunned for a moment—I couldn't believe what I had heard.

"What should I do?" I responded tentatively.

"Call the police," was her reply.

I had long suspected the enormity of my mother's inaction, but I loved her and didn't want to face her indifference to us kids. I didn't want her to be hurt. However, I didn't want to be hurt either. I realized I could not accomplish both.

"What would happen if I called the police?" I asked.

"The police would come to your house and talk to you and your parents. Most likely," the volunteer continued, "you would be removed from your home. How do you feel about that?"

"Nothing could be worse than living here," I replied determinedly.

The woman cautioned me what to expect. "Keep in mind, though, that the foster care system is overburdened, and you could easily land in an institutional sort of a home for girls."

"That's okay, too," I parried.

I was elated when I hung up the phone. I had someone who listened, understood, and believed me. I had found somewhere to go; someone to fight my battle. I felt a strange surge of power and purpose. Nobody could hurt me any more.

Mom returned home, still angry at my defiance and silent treatment. She tracked me down in the kitchen and addressed me in no uncertain terms.

"Now listen! Listen here, little Missy," she said harshly, "I'm not putting up with your nonsense. Who do you think you are? You're going to start talking to me and start talking now or you'll find out what real misery is."

Filled with this new feeling of having rights and being somebody. I replied firmly, "You're right, Mom, I'll talk. I have something to say. I just got off the phone with a volunteer worker from a teen-help hotline. I told her what goes on around here. She told me that Ed is an unfit parent, and that you are unfit for permitting him to hurt us. I was told to call the police and they would remove me from our house." I felt a strange sense of bravado as I looked at my mother.

Mom's mouth fell open. Horrified, she blurted out, "Oh, my God, did you give them your name?"

I had hoped in vain that Mom would rush to my rescue and say something like: "Oh, dear God, Nancy, I'm so sorry for what you've been through. I'll put a stop to this at once; I'll help. I'll be there for you!"

Instead I heard her outcry of: "Oh dear! What will happen to me? What will the neighbors think?"

Another betrayal.

Finally, Mom asked me in a desperate voice to give her a few minutes to think it over. She disappeared into her bedroom. When she emerged a moment later, she announced that she had made arrangements for me with the parents of my good friend, Lori Anderson. It was summer vacation time, the Anderson's were staying at their beach house, and I was invited to spend some time with them. Mom would take that interval to "straighten" things out. She would get rid of Ed.

I was thrilled. I loved my mother as most children love their mothers, and was ecstatic she was finally going to right this wrong.

Mom had informed the Andersons that I was having problems at home and everyone needed a break. After only two days, she drove up to their house.

She approached me, took me aside and told me point blank: "The Andersons don't like having you. You are a burden to them. I want you to come home."

When I refused to go home as long as Ed was still in the house, Mrs. Anderson, in turn, encouraged me to "try to get along with Ed."

"He is a nice man," she said, disregarding anything she might have heard to the contrary. "Every family has its problems. You just have to find a way to work out your difficulties."

Although the woman meant well, the advice pained me deeply, and I did not leave with my mother.

Over the years, many people refused to believe me; Ed's cruelty was beyond their comprehension. I have since learned that as long as the abusers and/or the family system continue to deny the abuse—people do not want to believe the victim. There is something in us that wants to disassociate from the truth. We don't want to taint ourselves with the horrible acts committed by individuals that we care about in our families and in our communities. Human nature is to deny the truth, protect our illusions and avoid unpleasantness.

The recent sexual abuse scandal in the Catholic Church demonstrates this well. As long as the offender denies the abuse, we want to believe him/her. It is difficult for parishioners to believe that wonderful "Father Joe" molested an altar boy; however, outside the parish, people are easily outraged.

Nevertheless, when we fail to investigate and/or believe the victim, we become complicit with the abuse.

A few days later, Mom again appeared at the Andersons unannounced and found me there alone. She demanded I return home.

"Is Ed still there?" I asked defiantly.

Mom replied, "Yes."

"Then I am not going home with you! I won't be hurt any more," I said with fierce determination.

An argument ensued and much to my amazement, Mom flew into a rage and screamed: "You fucking little bitch. I never want to see you again as long as I live."

She turned on her heels and walked towards the door in quick, angry strides, then abruptly stopped, looked back, and threw a bottle of Valium at me and yelled: "Here! Take them. You need them. You're sick!"

If someone had asked me how I felt at that moment, I would not have found the words to describe my feelings. I was numb. The hateful words she had flung at me burnt like acid in my soul. I knew I had lost and was lost. I sat down and sobbed. How devastating to be hated by one's own mother.

In the meantime, Mom convinced family, neighbors and friends alike that she was the unfortunate mother of a deeply troubled child. Everyone apparently believed her, while I suffocated under the heavy load of blame and shame, hopelessness and betrayal.

Three weeks later, Mom appeared again at the Andersons' home and informed me dispassionately that she had asked Ed to go his way.

That was all I wanted to hear. Peace and warmth rolled over me like a soft blanket on a freezing day, as I looked gratefully at my mother. This was too good to be true. I hurriedly packed my few things, thanked the Andersons profusely for letting me stay, hugged Lori, and followed Mom to the car. She had redeemed herself in my eyes. Life would be wonderful again. Mom loves me after all.

A week after I had come home, Ed, smug and strutting with his victory, returned to the family fold and took up where he left off.

By then, I abandoned the idea of calling in the authorities or asking for more help from the people at the teen hotline. I was convinced that no one would believe me and that all my relatives would hate me for causing so much trouble and dividing the family. No matter what I had attempted to do in the past to prevent or lessen the brutal punishments Ed was dishing out, nothing worked.

Feeling worthless and hurting, I plodded along numbly and prayed for a miracle.

As I had feared, life got worse. There wasn't a moment in the day or a special place in the house where I felt safe. Everyone was forever at each other's throat. I experienced daily the pain that filled our house, and I took upon myself the role of mediator. I wanted everyone to understand the other person's perspective and patiently interceded in arguments between my family members. Surprisingly, I often succeeded in settling the differences between Mom, Rob and Randy. Yet Mom was unable to do that for me. Without a parental figure to intercede on my behalf, I lived in emotional separation. The personal battles in our family raged on and the fights continued. The only way I could achieve a measure of peace was to acknowledge responsibility for every family difficulty. I couldn't do that. I suffered alone and in silence until my mind banished the unbearable pain to an unknown place. Disassociation was my constant childhood companion. My psyche extracted the feelings yet retained the memories. I've always had an extraordinary memory; I don't know why. However, I have

clear memories—both good and bad—as far back as the
age of three.

Around every corner, a new painful experience
awaited to test my emotional survival. One day, Ed asked
me to help him in the yard. I was petrified by that simple
request, because I knew that every time he asked us to do
a chore, something awful would happen. I dutifully
grabbed a rake and, complying obediently with Ed's instructions, began to rake the backyard alongside of him.

Rob's room faced the backyard. His window was open;
he was in his room reading. Ed had not requested his
presence for yard duty. Since I was in close proximity to the
house, I heard Mom enter Rob's room, asking him to put
his clean laundry away.

"I'll do it in a minute, Mom, I'm reading," Rob replied.

Mom's voice tightened as she demanded, "I want you
to do it now. Right now."

Rob snapped back, "I said, in a minute!"

Ed had heard, too. He dropped the rake, and in a flash
his whole being changed. The muscles in his lean, tall body
tensed, his nose narrowed, nostrils flared, the veins on his
neck and forehead bulged, and his eyes glassed over like
the marbled eyes of a goat. He breathed in harshly, mut-
tered threateningly under his breath, and tore toward the
house as though he was possessed.

I stood frozen, facing Rob's window, feet glued to the
grass beneath me. I knew what was coming.

First there came a terrifying crash and a loud thunk,
followed by horrifying sounds. It didn't seem possible that
the noise came from a human being. Rob screamed! He
screamed from his gut—deep guttural, low, raspy and raw

sounds. He was in agony! He sounded as though he was dying. I never have forgotten those screams.

The howling sounds of outraged humanity told the story I would later piece together from a bruised and beaten Rob. Ed had blown into his room with hurricane force, reached for Rob, pulled him down and threw him headfirst from his top bunk. He then lifted him off of the floor and repeatedly smashed his head against the wall before he whirled him around to hit his back against the sharp corner of the aquarium stand. When Rob tried to escape, Ed chased him around the room, hitting him in the stomach and wherever else his flailing fists could connect.

Finding it unbearable to witness any more of my brother's agony, I put myself into a trance. I remained standing still beneath the window and let the world drop away. I was in the middle of a big void. That's all there was—the void and the endless screams; that room and those sounds. The sheer walls of the protective void burst like a bubble when Ed's voice, screaming at the top of his lungs, cut through it.

"The next time you talk back to your mother, I'll beat you within an inch of your life!" Ed roared in uncontained fury.

As quickly as it had begun, the commotion stopped. I heard the sound of doors slamming shut, the revving of a car motor, and the squealing of wheels crunching on the cement driveway. Ed always took off after one of his performances, leaving us and the house broken and shattered, beaten and battered. He would return sometime later, calm and cool, acting as though nothing had happened.

In the silence of my world, I forced myself into action, got my feet into motion, and headed for the back door. The house made not a sound as it lay trapped in an eerie, discomforting silence. I felt as though I was walking in slow motion over a battlefield, sidestepping the remains of a terrible war. Like an old woman, afraid of what I was going to find, I climbed the stairs to my brother's room with concentrated effort, lifting one heavy foot after the other. I passed the closed door to my mother's room. I knew she was in there. What was she doing in there?

Rob's door was shut. I braced myself against what I knew I would find behind the door. I slowly turned the doorknob, and released the door just enough to slip through. My eyes were half-shut, not wanting to see. My worst fears matched the scene that greeted me.

The room was in shambles. Rob's desk lamp rested at a crazy angle on a pile of books and broken models that had been swept off of a shelf and littered the floor. A half-torn curtain fluttered limply in the breeze from the open window. School papers, posters and banners covered the floor and bunched up against the wall in silent protest.

Motionless, in the middle of it all lay Rob. He had been badly beaten. His face was blotchy and puffed up like a blowfish. Rivers of tears were silently streaking down his battered face. There was a dull glaze over his eyes, and behind the veil of tears lay a broken spirit.

I remained helplessly frozen to the spot near the door. My heart thumped in my throat, withered in sorrow and empathy that rose from the depth of my emotions. My eyes caught Rob's tear-filled look and left his face quickly as he turned his head slightly away from my gaze.

"Are you all right?" I asked in a hoarse whisper.

His jaw tightened and his chest convulsed slightly. His breath rasped as the words hissed from behind tightly clenched teeth, "I hate him." Slowly, with a long, low moan, trying not to add to the pain coursing through his bruised body, he turned away, and rolled over on his left side, silently staring at the blank wall.

After an emotion-filled pause, I managed a weak, "I know."

I gently closed Rob's door, went to my own room, plopped on my bed and sobbed bitter tears of helplessness, frustration and despair.

Would it ever stop? Would somebody have to be killed before something would be done?

Regardless of my misery, my anger and confusion, with childlike loyalty and later with adult devotion, I loved my mother, and doubted my own worthiness.

CHAPTER THREE

Whirlpool of Injustice and Betrayal

Rob and I had developed a love-hate relationship. As brother and sister we discussed our impossible situation, and on more than one occasion we fantasized about killing Ed. Rob and I also shared some close and touching moments. We often spoke lovingly, with a lost kind of hopeless longing, of our dead father. We clung to the past, recalled precious moments and the minutest things we remembered about him in our brief life with him. We wished fervently he had not left us and speculated at what life might have been had he not died. We shared each other's grief and understood each other's pain. At other times our relationship was very troubling.

The violent behavior patterns, the vile methods of disciplining for the imaginary infractions of the equally imaginary rules Ed employed, eventually made insidious inroads into our personalities as we acted out what we witnessed.

During a fun game of determining the winner by the process of elimination, the neighborhood kids tapped each other lightly on the back as they passed through a human tunnel as a sign of being "eliminated." When it was my turn, Rob yanked his belt out from around his waist and whipped me soundly. I was struck dumb as I turned to him shouting, "You whipped me! My own brother whipped me," I wailed, astonished beyond words.

Rob mimicked my painful outcries and added, with a mean grin on his face, "Ooohh, it was just a joke. Can't you take a joke?"

"I'll tell," I replied.

"Oh, no you won't. You know what Ed will do to me."

Rob had me coming and going. He could hurt me, because he knew I wouldn't tell on him because I didn't want him to get a beating.

One day Rob threw his body, shoulder first, into me for a little silly thing siblings usually settle with a bit of boisterous yelling and empty threats. I flew over a table, crashed onto the floor, and broke my ankle. Since telling on Rob would make me responsible for the beating he was sure to get, I preferred to hold my tongue and instantly became the butt of Ed's cruel remarks: I was clumsy, a klutz who couldn't walk a straight line across the living room floor. In order to save Rob from Ed's rage, I lied for him by saying I had tripped over the rug in the living room.

I was trapped in a vicious cycle. No matter how I moved, I would be sucked into the whirlpool of injustice and betrayal. If I told on Rob, I would have to watch him being beaten, and it would by my fault. If I didn't tell, Rob would have free rein to hurt me again.

Rob caught me unaware reading the newspaper and threw an orange at me. The orange burst through the paper and bounced off my face while he stood in front of me laughing hysterically. I snapped.

When Rob wouldn't leave me alone, I jumped up from my chair, and walked into the kitchen to get away from him. He followed me and we argued until he lunged at me to hit me. Instinctively, I reached for the meat cleaver Mom kept on the kitchen counter. I grabbed the sharp utensil in my upraised hands behind my head and yelled, "I'll kill you!"

Fear rose in his eyes and a terrified respect manifested in his rounded shoulders; Rob backed away from me without saying a word. It worked! He had taken me seriously. Finally, he realized that I had come to the end of my endurance. Yet the prospect of becoming as violent as the rest of my family terrified me.

On the one hand, I was afraid of Rob's frequent outbursts directed at me, which left me shaken and bruised, and on the other hand, I loved him and enjoyed our binding sibling camaraderie. We skied together, we socialized with mutual friends, and we managed to laugh conspiratorially at our lot in life, making Ed the butt of our hilarity. To lighten the load of living under an ever-present terror-charged atmosphere and to undermine Ed's importance as the head of the family—if only to ourselves—Rob and I, behind Ed's back, mimicked him to perfection. We had his tone of voice, grimaces, gestures and tirades down pat and replayed the most common and often repeated scenes to our own amusement, drowning out the pain of being the recipients of cruel and unjust punishment. Rob was a senior and drove me, a sophomore, to school every day. And like good buddies we helped each other out of trouble in our outside world.

I kept company with a few good friends, dated boys here and there, but had no special attachments to any of my dates. But then things changed. My mother met David on a skiing outing. Our family was well known at a local ski resort. Mom encountered David in the resort lounge and she integrated him into her crowd. For some reason, she introduced me to this older man. He quickly became my steady companion. Several years my senior, he was funny, carefree and sure of himself. He seemed quite unconcerned with Ed's abrasive behavior and the man's obvious expressions of dislike for David's presence. I became fond of David and we spent a lot of time together. We got to know each other well in spite of Ed's open display of disapproval.

That spring, Mom appeared restless and subdued. Whatever was troubling her remained a secret. One gray and rainy afternoon when we had gathered in the living room after school, Mom dropped the bomb.

"I'm divorcing Ed. He's moving out," she declared.

Surprise, relief and curiosity surged through me and made my heart skip a beat or two. Before I sorted out my feelings, I wondered briefly what had occurred for Mom to make this decision.

Rob later confided in me that Mom had witnessed his last beating from Ed. She stood in the doorway and watched as Ed beat him silly, before retreating to her room. It was on that day she "woke up," realizing Ed could literally kill one of her children. She had made her plans in secret, sharing them only with Rob, shortly after the terrible beating he had received from Ed.

Although I was elated that Ed was leaving, I felt hurt that Mom was willing to leave Ed for Rob's sake, however, months earlier she was unwilling to leave him to protect me.

To add insult to injury, when Mom confided in Rob her plans to leave Ed, she instructed him to keep her plans a secret from me. "Nancy always interferes in my marriage and I don't want her to change my plans this time," she complained.

When people are in this kind of delusion and denial, they tend to thrust responsibility for their dilemmas and decisions on to others. Not only did Mom partner with Rob in an unhealthy fashion, she collaborated with him again to assign me a power that I didn't have, leaving me feeling responsible for her choices. However, I didn't possess the power to formulate Mom's marital decisions at twelve years old when she instructed me to ask Ed to stay. I didn't hold the power to make Ed leave when I was fifteen years old and I refused to come home from the Anderson's as long as Ed was there, and I didn't have nor did I want the power to make her marital decisions on this day.

Stripped of his autocratic powers and no longer the reigning terror, Ed carried on like a baby in front of us, whining and crying, pleading and begging, to no avail. He packed his bags and left our lives for good. Relieved and delighted as I was at his departure, I couldn't help sympathizing with his pain. I always related to the pain of others; I had become numb and unaware of my own.

Naive and optimistic, I had great hopes that life would become wonderful with Ed out of the picture. Freed from the oppressive tyrant, I envisioned our family becoming the loving, happy unit it had been years ago. Now we would have fun again, enjoy each other, be kind to each other, and be a real family.

But things had gone too far down the road of destructive behavior. The careless handling of respect and dignity for each other had deteriorated the possibilities of recapturing any semblance of peaceful "normal" conditions.

Whatever expectations I had for our future did not materialize. We were left to our own devices.

Mom was blithely unaware of our needs and was guided by her own interests. She pursued her ambitions and pleasures, which were divided between working and dating. She wasn't around to bring the much-needed order and cohesiveness into our lives.

I confided in my best friend, Lori, that everything was a mess and everybody just went wild. I discussed my preoccupation with suicide with her, and she patiently talked me out of that notion by pointing out how selfish an act it was. Being selfish caused someone else pain, I rationalized, and I most certainly couldn't do that. Life went on and changed daily, presenting me with constant demands and challenges to adjust and accommodate. I spent some time in the company of schoolmates, but I missed being with my special friend, David.

By then David's company transferred him to California, and I yearned for his jovial company. He wrote frequently, and his letters added a ray of light to my life. Another big change occurred when Rob moved into his own apartment. In spite of leaving the nest, we continued to do things together. We double-dated, went skiing, and spent weekends at the cabin. I kept up with school and my friends, and buried deep within my heart all my broken dreams and tarnished expectations for a harmonious family life—mother, brothers and myself.

Within months, Mom had a new man in her life. Bill was a practicing alcoholic, had a sour view of the world, and was highly critical of the people he met. He set off all my warning bells, and he of course, liked nothing about me and let me know his opinions in no uncertain terms. Mom and I started quarreling bitterly. She told me out flat that Bill was her first priority and his treatment of me was inconsequential.

My observations and appraisals of Bill led me to warn Mom that he was all wrong. But she got angry at me for butting in on her life, and told me I was cruel.

I knew that it was all starting all over again.

Feeling unwanted and unloved, I found my life unbearable and wanted a way out. I missed David. I talked to Rob. He was practical. "You're three-quarters of the way through your senior year. Transfer your credits to California. You can move in with David and graduate from high school there," he advised. "I'll help you with the move," he offered.

No sooner said than done, I was on my way. Today, as I look back at that period in my life, I am convinced that had I stayed at home, I would either have self-destructed or taken my own life.

But I didn't leave home with a light heart. On the contrary. My grandmother accused me of hurting my mother. Other relatives accused me of being an ungrateful child. Mom said I was mean and cruel and had hurt her deeply. Still impressionable and my spirits tottering under the load of the pain from the past, I accepted the notion that I was that selfish and ungrateful daughter, careless of my mother's feelings.

I left home and, along with my several pieces of luggage, I carried a load of guilt and remorse so big that it didn't fit in any suitcase. I had barely room for it in my heart.

CHAPTER FOUR

New Beginnings

Your future depends on many things, but mostly on you.
—Frank Tyger

California was sunny and warm. Instead of the traditional puffed-up, silvery-gray overcast of the northern Washington weather scene, blue skies washed in California-gold sunlight were one of the immediate rewards I embraced.

The new school, life with David, getting to know a strange town, no old friends about, all brought their share of loneliness into my life. But the past had made an emotional loner out of me at a young age.

Morro Bay was considerably smaller than bustling Seattle and the faces of the young people I met at school reflected the carefree innocence of an untroubled childhood, and a seemingly less complicated time of growing into adulthood than I had experienced. I made myself fit my surroundings in a quiet and unobtrusive way. When it was time to graduate, I did so without family and fanfare.

For quite a while, I tucked away the past along with my heart and made-believe all was well in my world. My mind activated a compartment in my memory labeled "convenient," and I remembered only the good and fun things from my childhood. I convinced myself I had a loving, normal family in Seattle. With David, I shared my animated repertoire of a string of hilarious stories from long ago.

We had a rollicking good time laughing at the innocence and joys of childhood where shadows were merely misunderstood monsters, frightening apparitions were billowing curtains filled by a mischievous summer night breeze, and where loving parents guided Easter bunnies, good fairies, and Santa Claus to the right address.

I went about building a new life for myself with David at my side. There were new surroundings, new jobs, and a new set of friends. Without the day-to-day presence of my family as a reminder, it seemed easy to forget the past hurts and bask in the safety of the present. But no matter where I went, there were certain things I could not leave behind. Occasionally, I displayed signs of post-traumatic stress disorder but was unaware of its significance.

Whenever a terror-ridden flashback threatened the sanity and safety of my life and I tried to tell David, he not only did not want to understand my distress, but discouraged any further attempts to make him a partner to my concerns. Neither one of us knew what post-traumatic stress meant. I accepted his stand. If some of my behavior seemed odd and bizarre at times, neither he nor I paid attention to it.

Sometimes, such as when David and I moved into our new home, these episodes were hard to miss. As I came out of the front door of our new house, I encountered David. He was loaded down with a heavy television set heading up the narrow porch towards the front door. I was startled by David's sudden appearance. I glanced up quickly and thought I saw Ed rather than David. Instinctively—born out of an unknown fear—I panicked. Instead of stepping to the side to give David room to pass me. I wildly leaped over the porch railing, down a small embankment and landed with a thud in the soft dirt of the ground beneath. I was petrified. I didn't know what was happening to me.

I may have made a geographic change, adopted a completely new and different lifestyle, and disassociated myself from everything that was unpleasant, painful and disturbing—but, basically, nothing had changed of course. Certain situations triggered terrible feelings in me which I was unable to connect to an incident. I knew that the sight of a dirty dish or a used glass was highly uncomfortable to me, but I didn't know why.

Sometimes I remembered an incident from my past but was not able to feel the horror of it. Not being able to connect incidents with reactions or feelings with a happening, left me bewildered and confused.

Many years later, I did come to terms with my Post-Traumatic Stress Disorder.

Occasionally, my mind still convinces me that an unimaginable disaster looms just around the corner. I can spend days, living "on edge" with feelings of unknown impending doom until I "shake myself" and remember that my fear is just my companion PTSD. This realization calms my nerves and reminds me that my fear is in the past and that I am safe in the present.

I was terribly disappointed when Mom called to tell me she had married Bill. I was discouraged because Bill further threatened the fragile relationship with my mother and added to my growing concerns for Randy's as well as Mom's physical and emotional well-being.

Over the next four years, I would see my mother on only four separate occasions. Each time I was aware that things just weren't right. I felt a familiar tension in her house and sensed that Bill was physically abusing Randy as well as my mother. My brother wasn't talking, and Mom denied my concerns and became irritated at my interference.

During one of my few visits home, Mom gave birth to a baby boy, Brandon. I stopped at the hospital to meet my new brother. As I looked at the tiny bundle, I couldn't help but wonder just what was in store for this little newcomer. The visit with Mom had a perfunctory air about it, our parting was colorless, dull and void of emotion.

Randy visited me that summer, and David and I took my then fourteen-year-old brother all over California and showed him the best time. His behavior was a clue of what was going on with him. Although unconfirmed at the time, he was now the victim of Bill's physical and emotional abuse. Randy carried the legacy of fear and emotional upheaval on his young shoulders. Although polite and well-mannered, he acted like a nervous old man.

He worried constantly and required a steady flow of reassurance that all was well and he was safe. When he left for Seattle, I was deeply concerned. When I called my family and voiced my worries, Mom laughed it off. Rob and my grandmother became upset and accused me of repeatedly "stirring the pot." Everyone denied the presence of abuse at Mom's house, and became angry with me when I brought it up. With no concrete proof, I dropped the matter.

In the ensuing years, my family continued to batter me emotionally into silence. Silence damages the victim and only serves to nourish the abuse and shield the wrongdoer from accountability. Simply put—silence aids the abuser.

David and I married and one year later, I discovered to my and David's delight that I was pregnant. I felt great, had a normal pregnancy, and when I held my first-born daughter, Tara, in my arms, joy soared through me and sang its very own special song of fulfillment and wonder. I looked at my daughter with awe. The baby was so tiny, so innocent and so vulnerable. A new fear gripped me as I tried to fathom the vast responsibility, wise guidance and parental protection it would take to raise a healthy, whole human being.

Looking at my baby, I could feel the old pain of my own childhood casting a dark shadow over this golden day. I held the tiny bundle of life close to my body as I sat alone in my hospital room and addressed the world at large, "Nobody is ever going to hurt you. Nobody!" I promised fiercely. "And," I added in a soft whisper, "especially not I."

After my father's death, I spent my growing up years and into adulthood challenging our abuse. I knew I had to make a conscious decision to learn a healthy method of parenting. As soon as I realized I was pregnant, I devoured parenting books, took parenting classes, surrounded myself with people whose parenting skills I respected and admired and drew off of my earlier memories and experiences with my father. Dad bestowed upon me his loving parental heart. These intentional choices on my part marked the beginning of breaking the cycle of family violence with respect to my own children.

Mom called to ask if she could come to California. She announced she was divorcing Bill and needed a vacation.

After her arrival, she sheepishly admitted that I had been right in my appraisal of him.

"Bill is an alcoholic," she confessed, her voice becoming high-pitched and shrill. "I found out he beat his mother before she died. He beat me. He beat Randy. He pinched my face purple and called me a bitch." The list of insults, beatings and batterings was endless while my mind raced. I had been right. My worst fears had finally been validated with the truth.

To my amazement, Mom examined the mistakes she had made after the death of my father right out loud. She referred to Ed and Bill as monsters. She even recalled the unflattering statement her attorney had made when she went to him to start divorce proceedings against Bill. The lawyer told her to find another attorney; he wouldn't work for her if she kept marrying and divorcing abusive men. He suggested she'd better stick with the man she had.

When she told all, she complained that she never knew how to handle a family without the guidance of her husband. She said that she needed help in raising her three children.

I had conflicting emotions and observations about Mom and straddled the fence in surprise and concern. I felt sorry for her. I believed that she was merely a "victim" of ignorance and was coming to terms with her "mistakes." I believed that I had the beginning and the promise for a "real" relationship with my mother.

CHAPTER FIVE

Struggling to Forgive

After more than five moves in five years, and an offer pending from David's company to move again, this time to Los Angeles, I objected. Not only didn't I want to live in Los Angeles, but if he stayed with his company, David could count on being constantly moved from pillar to post, and I wanted some permanency. I felt disconnected and without roots.

Naively, I argued that living close to my family and old friends would give me the stability and the roots I needed. We agreed to move to Seattle. David would leave his company and strike out on his own. Tara was almost a year old when we left California and headed for Washington.

Grandma and Grandpa had invited us to stay with them until we could get settled in our own house. It was a childlike homecoming for me. I seized every opportunity that might bring me closer to attaining the motherly love I so passionately sought.

Happy as a kid in a candy store to be "back home" again, I went to see Mom before I even unpacked my bags. I checked my image briefly in the mirror. Satisfied, I danced out of the house and bounced into the car with youthful verve, brimming over with uncontained anticipation of seeing my mother again.

I pulled up in front of the familiar house, hurriedly turned off the motor, and barely took time to slam the car door shut. I flew up the sidewalk and knocked on the door. It was locked. When Mom answered the door, it took but a second to dash my joyous expectations and shatter my dreams into a thousand jagged and useless shards. Mom looked at me coldly, her eyes displaying an unmasked annoyance.

"I don't have time to see you," she said. "You can't expect me to drop everything to spend time with you. I have a life of my own. I'm going to school. I take care of Brandon and the house, and you're intruding," she added, anger rising in her voice.

Stunned and devastated, but hiding my hurt and swallowing my pride, I pleaded with her, "Mom, you're important to me. I haven't seen you in a long time, and I would like to spend some time with you." I didn't understand what had changed since the last time I saw her.

Mom's answer was a long tirade of astonishing charges and accusations. She recalled her versions of incident after incident of what she felt I had done by bringing chaos into her life.

"I resent the things you have done," she began in a querulous tone of voice. "When you were only twelve years old, you made my decisions for me and made me stay married to Ed. We could have been rid of him, but because of you, I stayed married to him years longer than I should have!"

"You asked me to go to him and beg him to stay," I managed to interject, not believing what I heard.

"I've been seeing a therapist since I left Bill, and even he says you shouldn't have been making my decisions for me. I resent that you did," she retorted angrily.

"Mom, I was a child. I did what you told me to do. I was not the bad guy. I was the victim," I blurted out.

But Mom didn't hear a word I said.

"I was the victim!" she angrily stated. "I was as power-less as you. How dare you to have made my decisions?"

Mom continued to rage against me bringing up a long list of childhood grievances, assigning me with the respon-sibility for her seven-year marriage to Ed.

I left Mom's house stripped, whipped, naked, and destroyed. I got behind the wheel of my car and drove back to my grandparent's house. I was numb.

Mom called Grandma and told her what had hap-pened.

Grandma admonished me for being selfish and told me to change my attitude.

"Why can't you be nice to your mother?' She asked in a pained voice. "Must you contribute to her problems?" she continued.

"Your mother has had a rough life," Grandmother pleaded her daughter's case. "You should feel sorry for her instead of making things tougher for her. Bill was mean and cruel and much worse than Ed. The problem with you Nancy, is you're not forgiving," she concluded.

I stood in stunned silence.

Grandma blamed me for hurting my mother and told me to forgive her without ever acknowledging any of the abuse. This caused a self-depreciating internal turmoil. I too, believed on a human and a spiritual level that I should forgive. I wanted to live with the peace that comes from forgiveness. I did not understand why forgiveness seemed so self-destructive. I have since learned that forgiveness does not protect us from past, present and future abuse. It would be many years before I learned that I needed to have the abuse acknowledged before I could forgive. People were asking me to do the impossible and I felt like a bad person because I could not achieve the forgiveness that was beyond my reach. I experienced others demands to forgive Mom without acknowledging her offenses as another form of abuse.

Full of pain and looking for understanding, I turned to David for comfort. But David didn't know how to deal with my pain.

"Oh, Nancy, it's no big deal. Don't let it bother you," he advised.

There was neither support nor understanding when I turned to others for aid. My pain deepened when friends and family members insisted that I must forgive, forget and simply get along with my mother. When people made statements such as, "You know you only have one mother," or "You'll live to regret making negative remarks about your mother…" these comments suggested condoning abuse and reinforced the fact that a mother is a mother regardless of her actions. All the responsibility for a "normal" relationship with my mother was portrayed as one sided; it was mine and mine alone.

A feeling of complete loneliness and despair engulfed my being. I didn't know where to turn. The only way for me to survive with some dignity and recapture a corner of my sanity was to shut down the compartment that contained the painful memories, the insults, and the lies. Once again I shifted gears.

David and I bought a house, and excited, we moved into our new home. I thoroughly enjoyed Tara and was thrilled when I discovered that I was pregnant again. I gave birth to another beautiful baby girl. We named her Dawn.

During the next several years, I desperately sought to resolve the inner turmoil that kept me on the edge and would not let up. My marriage to David deteriorated rapidly as my need for intimacy crashed head on with his need for solitude. At this point, I finally realized that David had "rescued" me from my abuse. Yet, I needed more—I needed emotional growth. We tried couple counseling as we struggled to hold our marriage together. Aside from couple counseling, I independently entered therapy to address my childhood issues. My therapist, however, was unqualified in the field of abuse, and didn't help.

I was twenty-five years old, when in my constant search for answers to my mixed emotions and remedies for my charred feelings; I came across a book by Harold Bloomfield, M.D., titled, *Making Peace with Your Parents*.

"Making peace with your parents is a personal challenge that will bring you enormous and lasting satisfaction," promised Dr. Bloomfield, and I was all for it.

If forgiving means healing, and being healed means the lifting of the unbearable load stored for years in my fragile inner being, so be it. In a thorough and methodical way, I studied the book carefully from cover to cover and followed instructions and directions to a T. I used the recommended exercise of going from resentment to forgiveness and forced myself to believe I was not hurt intentionally. I learned clever ways to express anger and love at the same time. I acquired the prescribed set of expressions and verbiage to convey my new approach to the old problem.

In fact, I truly felt bad Mom had been a victim of her men, of circumstances, and the cruel ways of life in general. With this new information simmering in my mind, I made a sincere and genuine effort to forgive and turned a blind eye to the abuse which continued in the inner family circle. I understood that I couldn't change my mother, so I changed myself. I made peace.

I didn't realize at the time that I felt battered into forgiveness. Enduring forgiveness cannot be achieved if it is forced, or attempted without receiving acknowledgment of the abuse. Authentic forgiveness is born out of love—a love that begins with oneself and lives in harmony with spirit. I had much to learn before I could accomplish this.

I wrote Mom a beautiful letter, to which Mom replied graciously, expressing a wish to have lunch with me. We met for lunch and made an attempt at conversation, discussing everything from weather to clothes. Finally, I guided the conversation to what was uppermost in my heart. Facing Mom squarely, I spoke in the most loving and gentle way.

"Mom, I forgive you," I said softly.

Mom's eyes instantly filled with fury, and she snapped, "That makes me very angry. I've done nothing to be forgiven for."

I uttered a silent "Ouch" to myself, yet continued to prescribe to the formula of forgiveness. Surely, it would work in time.

Our mother-daughter lunch had come to an end.

Superficially, Mom and I had finally achieved a harmonious coexistence, just like everyone else in the family. I personified the loving daughter, played the gracious hostess at family gatherings, and got along well with everyone. Silently, I endured Mom's constant insults and criticisms while fights and arguments came to a screeching halt, and the rest of the family nodded in pleased recognition of the change that had come over Nancy, the troublemaker.

The next decade brought the sad but foreseeable end to my marriage to David and a short-lived subsequent marriage. The years also brought more abusive marriages and relationships for Mom.

Early in this period of time, Brandon had grown into a healthy, happy young boy, and my baby brother's troubles didn't start until Mom announced she was getting married to a man named Lou. I knew little if anything about Mom's new husband.

Unfortunately, I couldn't stay away from my mother. In my driving need to have a relationship with her, like a moth to the light, I was forever drawn into her affairs. I was the eternal bystander, victim, and witness to the turmoil and abuse which had once again become a daily occurrence.

When I tried to let Mom know how disturbed I was by Lou's mean and abusive behavior toward Brandon, she replied in exasperation, "Nancy, why do I always have trouble with you? Only you? Never the boys! You're sick and a troublemaker!"

Wanting the love of my mother was not a passing desire, but rather a universal need as old as humankind. I needed the love and support of a mother. Through the ages we have placed our mothers on pedestals of honor and devotion. She is the person we depend on as helpless infants, the one we rely on and lean on to guide us through childhood, and who should bear with us as we awkwardly stumble into adulthood. She is the model we are supposed to fashion ourselves after, the friend we are supposed to have for life.

She is the center of our universe, the provider of all the childhood magic and miracles; the one being we rely on and love the most. She is also the one person who can hurt us more than anybody else.

I wanted my mother's love so desperately, I didn't even realize that I did not—and should not trust her.

Trust is such a basic relationship necessity that if we can't trust a parent to love and protect us—whom can we trust? When we have been betrayed in our most basic human relationship—and that trust is never restored— how can we learn to trust ourselves to respond appropriately to betrayal? I struggle to this day with these questions.

I actually betrayed myself when I accepted betrayal as a part of my relationship with my mother.

No matter how hard I worked on our relationship, I didn't feel loved by my mother.

It drove me insane that she couldn't see what was happening. Why couldn't she see I loved her and wanted a relationship with her?

Mom and I were at an impasse. I believed abuse to be "the problem." Mom believed my expressions of dislike for abuse to be "the problem." However, the actual "problem" was betrayal—Mom's betrayal of her children and my self-betrayal as an adult.

I kept thinking, if I could just get her to see the abuse, she would love me.

Each time I tried to approach Mom, I felt I was walking on eggshells and tried, oh so carefully and lovingly, to point out Brandon was hurting and needed help. No matter how gentle my approach, Mom would attack and call me a never-ending range of hurtful names.

Her caustic statements sent me into a tailspin. Ripping open old wounds, old memories threatened my emotional well-being, and caused countless hours of concern for my young brother. I couldn't stand to see him hurt as I had been. Approaching Mom never worked. When I voiced my concerns to the rest of the family, their insults added to my injuries and silenced me in my effort to bring the truth to light. Everyone told me to butt out.

When we are in the midst of our behavioral patterns, they are difficult for us to identify. As I said before, children are taught how to process the information they gather from their experiences.

At this point, I hadn't learned my part in our continued family cycle. Although I knew our family functioned in a very unhealthy manner, I didn't know what was healthy. Nurturing family relationships were outside my realm of experience.

If Mom had protected us as children, we would have been safe from our abuse. Further, if Rob had understood that it was Mom's responsibility to protect us—not mine—I would have been safe from his misplaced rage. I spent my childhood trying to convince Mom and Rob of these facts. In reality, if they had understood this information, I would have been safe.

My family constantly drilled into my head, until it was ingrained in me and on some level I believed it myself, that I should be silent and that all the family difficulties were my fault. Therefore, as an adult I continued to argue over our protection. I didn't realize at the time, that I had different choices as an adult than I did as I child. I was no longer dependant on Mom for our protection.

As an adult, I still needed to learn that, unlike in childhood, I had the power to protect my youngest brother and myself. I continued to look to the very person who harmed us for help and validation. Without validation from anyone else—I couldn't see—much less break this pattern. Unfortunately, this childhood model followed me for years, not only in my family of origin, but also in the other significant relationships in my adult life.

When I left Mom's house and closed the front door behind me, a battle raged within my tortured mind. On one hand, I was clinging to Dr. Bloomfield's forgive-and-keep-loving doctrine about making peace with one's parents. On the other hand, I was puzzled and confused by just why I felt so lousy, so depressed, and so ready to be so, so unforgiving.

Years later, Andrew Vachss, attorney and author, stated in an article in *Parade* Magazine in August 1994, "Emotional abuse is the cruelest and longest lasting of all." He goes on to say, "When your self-concept has been shredded, when you have been deeply injured and made to feel that the injury was all your fault, when you look for approval to those who cannot or will not provide it—you play the role assigned to you by your abusers. It's time to stop."

Vachss, who has devoted his life to protecting children, further states that for the emotionally abused child, in the end ... "healing comes down to forgiving yourself—knowing you deserve to be respected, you deserve to be loved."

Brandon went through all kinds of nightmares as Lou drank and declared himself the law of the land. However, his reign came to a quick end when drunk, cursing and bumping around the house, he discharged a gun in Mom's direction. Mom called the police, and her fourth marriage ended.

CHAPTER SIX

Mother, I Am Angry

More dangerous than anger and hate is indifference.
To be indifferent to suffering is what makes the human being
inhuman. It is not a beginning, it is an end, and it is always
the friend to the enemy.
—Elie Wiesel

At thirty-three years of age, I still loved outdoor activities, remained an enthusiastic participant in all kinds of sports, and worked out regularly. A voracious reader, I was able to express myself clearly and eloquently. I had many friends and held a responsible position in a fast-growing company. It appeared that I had the world by the tail.

Yet, nothing had changed on the inside of me.

By then, Mom had selected a new man. Smokey was cut from the same cloth as her previous mates. He was offensive in his manners, he "ran" the show, overstepped his authority with my daughters and me, was rude and crude; and, more than that, he abused thirteen-year-old Brandon.

I met Smokey days after he and Mom started dating. The girls were away with their father for the weekend. Brandon, Mom and I agreed to meet at Lake Roesiger before going to the fair together.

The scene that greeted me at Mom's cabin was instantly uncomfortable and eerily familiar to the past. Smokey didn't want to leave until the football game was over. He barked out orders, complaints and insults as Brandon waited impatiently to leave. Each time my young brother walked near Smokey, the man reached out and smacked the side of Brandon's head with the back of his hand. Mom refused to even look up from her newspaper as Brandon pleaded with her for help.

I watched in horror—re-living my own childhood experiences of Mom's detached silence.

We stopped at a little market on the way to the fair. Mom went inside the store while Smokey, Brandon and I waited for her in the car. Brandon leaned forward and turned on the radio. Smokey immediately changed the station. When Brandon reached for the radio again, Smokey grabbed his hand and bent his fingers back. Brandon yelled, "Ouch! Ouch! Ouch!" Smokey laughed. My whole body tensed. I knew Mom and I were going to clash again over the abusive behavior of another man.

My young brother telephoned frequently to confide his miseries to me. He suffered from an all-encompassing range of emotional abuse. Smokey tormented him; constantly belittled Brandon and controlled his every move. This new man nonchalantly referred to Brandon as "asshole" rather than by his name. Brandon's repeated complaints to Mom fell on deaf ears. She either ignored him with deliberate silence, laughed it off, or blamed Brandon.

I was totally stunned at the repetition and continuation of the abusive cycle that never ended. I listened to Brandon and validated his feelings. He told Mom he didn't like the way Smokey treated him. As supporting evidence, he told her that I had agreed he was being mistreated. Mom would have rather I ignored him. She was adamant that Smokey's treatment of Brandon was not inappropriate, but that my validating his feelings and undermining her was unacceptable. I understood she didn't know how to stand up to or even recognize the abuse her partners dispensed, and felt I was trying to turn my brother against her. She interpreted my efforts to uncover and end the abuse as attempts to turn the family against her. In an attempt to deny reality and to have our lives remain as "status quo," everyone else agreed my actions were cruel and worse, for they were undermining Mom. However, I simply wanted the abuse to end and everyone to get along.

I was out of my mind with fear for my youngest brother's well-being and I was torn between keeping the peace in the family and intervening on Brandon's behalf. I was frantic! For twenty-five years, I had tried everything to change things and had failed. For twenty-five years, I had been emotionally bashed by the members of my family for my efforts. The whole family had turned on me, threatening to withhold their love unless I changed. They labeled me a troublemaker.

I felt hopeless, helpless and terribly frightened. Like a fast car spinning its wheels on loose gravel, I was fast losing control. I had countless recurring nightmares from which I awakened screaming silently into the dark night. Weak and covered in perspiration, I would straighten the tangled bed sheets, trying to dispel the frightening scenes with which my mind had invaded the much-needed rest. Slowly as my shaking subsided, I'd settle back against the smoothed-out pillow, attempting to banish the monsters from inside my head for the remainder of the night. In the clear of day, groping for answers and solutions, I opted once again to find a therapist.

Through all this, I poured myself into the care of the girls, jealously guarding their well-being and providing them with a safe and loving environment. I delighted in their healthy, sturdy bodies and minds, as I watched them turning from little girls into adolescence, making all my efforts pay off by becoming happy, "normal" kids.

Having been so misunderstood and "unheard" as a child, I made sure my children knew they were loved and had a mother who listened and understood them. I set guidelines for the girls and tempered discipline with a lighthearted and relaxed approach to establishing values and dealing with problems real and imagined. There would be no carry-over of fear and terror for them!

Trying to "forgive" my mother may have resulted in a more comfortable relationship on a purely social level, but it had done nothing to ease my pain, nor did it put the past and present abuse to rest. My efforts of convincing Mom and the family that I was no longer a troublemaker ended the fighting, and no one else seemed upset with me. But it was a solely superficial gesture, no different than putting a bandage over a wound caused by a splinter without removing the offending piece of wood.

It was at this point that I tried to prevent Brandon's abuse without being destroyed myself. I desperately wanted to help my brother, but did not want the family to mutilate me in the process.

As adults, my brothers and I responded to abuse just as we had as children. Randy became "invisible" and moved out of state permanently. I was the "troublemaker," trying to prevent the continued cycle of abuse of family members. And Rob was Mom's protector. He attacked me viciously when I tried to prevent the past from repeating itself over and over again.

Finally, I went to see Mom and lovingly asked her to protect Brandon. Characteristically, my mother was furious with me.

I stood my ground. "Mom," I said firmly, "I'm not afraid of you anymore and I will do anything to protect Brandon. Every time I've tried to prevent abuse, you've called in the family for reinforcement to shut me up. You've made me out as a crazy and a troublemaker. But I'm not backing down this time!"

Mom denied my accusations vehemently and reminded me once again that I was sick and the one with the real problem.

Looking for support and reinforcement on Brandon's behalf, I spoke with Randy, but he said I was out of line in going to our mother. After all, Mom had a heart condition and shouldn't have to handle any more problems. Besides, Mom wasn't the problem. The men in her life were.

"Leave her alone," Randy instructed, "I'll take care of Brandon."

He did nothing of the kind.

During a phone call to Rob, I again asked for his help in protecting Brandon.

"What do you mean? How dare you tell me Brandon is being abused?" he challenged, shouting across the wires.

"People have been chained and whipped since the beginning of time," he continued to rant and rave. "The human race has survived; we survived; he'll survive. I happen to be proud of myself and my family. You! You are sick and weak and unstable. You live in fantasy land. You always have and you always will." He hung up on me.

I was shocked and stunned. I clutched the receiver in my hand listening to dead air. I shuddered as another door slammed shut in my face. Imprisoned by silence, my emotions turned to slush. I sat motionless on the edge of my bed and stared vacantly into space.

At the time, I could not comprehend why my brothers became so angry whenever I mentioned the abuse. I have since come to understand their fear. We all lost our father when we were very young. The thought of losing our mother as well, was intolerable. Mom's love was conditional on accepting the abuse. My brothers did not have the courage to risk losing Mom's love, by facing the damage her betrayal had done to us. I was already aware that I did not have my mother's unconditional love.

Moments passed. I straightened my back, squared my shoulders, and pulled myself together. My mind began working again, and my thoughts turned to the problem at hand.

I was angry! Angry at myself! Why had I even tried to forgive my mother? I had been cheated, betrayed, and ripped off! Here was my mother—four abusive relationships later, and she hadn't changed an iota. She hadn't said she was sorry for allowing me to be abused or for another one of her children to be mistreated. Instead she blamed me for making trouble! Suddenly, I no longer cared about mending my relationship with her. In all these years, all attempts at reconciliation had come from me.

During the five years I lived in California, Mom didn't as much as send me a birthday card. I thought about our connection. It was based almost solely on abuse. Ninety-five percent of the time I spent with my mother she threw emotional garbage at me. I wasn't getting anything good out of this association. All I did was "hang out" to make sure Brandon and my girls weren't getting hurt. I remained adamant about protecting Brandon, even though I didn't know how I could make it happen.

I didn't know how to help my brother and unfortunately, I still didn't know how to help myself.

Even though I knew I was angry, I didn't know it was okay to be angry. Merely stating the obvious was not enough. I didn't learn until much later how to resolve my rage. This required intensive work, researching various methods of appropriately directing my anger towards my mother.

It is important to note my complete inability to identify my own feelings. Feeling my anger and sadness were beyond my comprehension. These were skills I didn't learn as a child and didn't even know I lacked. For example: When a child smashes a finger in the doorway and cries out in pain, a parent generally gives an empathic response such as, "Oh sweetie, that really hurts," and proceeds to comfort the child. The child learns how to feel hurt and sad. They learn from their parents and others to internalize these feelings for themselves. I didn't experience these responses as a child. As just one example: In the limousine on the way to my father's grave-side services, I started to cry. My mother slapped me and told me to stop crying. I lacked a model to show me how to feel compassion for my pain.

When our feelings are denied as children, we develop an emotional disconnect. Although I was taught and learned to have compassion for the feelings of others, I was unable to recognize my own hurt.

When we don't learn these basic skills as children, we need to learn them as adults. The problem is identifying the skills we have never learned and therefore, we don't know we are lacking.

Self-compassion is such a basic skill, I instinctively taught it to my own children. Yet, I failed to recognize I didn't have it for myself. After I did recognize I lacked self-compassion, I didn't know how to learn. How do you "re-parent" yourself? Even if you know how to parent someone else—that doesn't mean you know how to parent yourself.

Later in counseling, my therapist told me I needed to get angry and mourn. Instructing me to feel powerful emotions was not enough in my case. Years later, another therapist understood that I literally needed to be taught the same way a child is taught. She explained how to seek out people to receive empathic responses until I could internalize them for myself. In childhood as well as adulthood, each time I shared my feelings with someone, the chosen confidant denied my perceptions. Since I wasn't accustomed to relationships with people who would acknowledge the way I felt, I didn't understand the experience of receiving empathy, or that I could even successfully seek empathy.

Until people taught me what it felt like to be self-compassionate, I didn't know that a wide range of emotions existed for me and were necessary to help me protect myself and others.

I didn't learn until I was much older that I had a right to my feelings. I needed to own my anger, sadness and fear without permission from anyone else. I continued to seek permission from my family to feel outraged. When they told me I was "sick" and didn't give me the permission I needed, I argued for the right to feel the way I did, rather than knowing I had the right to feel angry.

I remained "stuck" in one place. I needed to own my pain in order to resolve my anger and grow emotionally. This growth was a prerequisite to protect my brother, and myself.

My several attempts to find answers, release and relief in counseling sessions had all ended in dismal failures. Still, I knew that there had to be someone who could help me.

* * * * *

As I sat across from Thomas for the first time, I was a bit apprehensive and looked for signs to indicate just what kind of therapist and person he was. I didn't trust easily and was more than skittish about putting my welfare into someone's hands.

However, I felt comfortable at once in his presence. I sensed a quiet strength in the man, commanding yet compassionate. His face reflected serenity and purpose. His voice was nice and strong.

I began the initial session by telling him about my childhood. Story after story poured out of me, punctuated by vivid descriptions and harrowing details of the violent acts which crowded my childhood days. Interestingly enough, most of the incidents I related to Thomas concerned the mistreatment of my brothers. I was vague and uncertain about my own experiences.

I had been conditioned to down play my own abuse, and even though I depicted harrowing stories about Ed's role in the household, I never examined the gravity of the situation.

"You know," I said slowly, "there is a difference between being punished for doing something wrong, or being brutalized because it makes someone else feel good. We were punished because Ed liked it! And my mother stood by and let it happen," I observed.

Thomas just nodded his head in agreement, and then suggested I write a letter to myself as a child and address those painful issues.

I was amazed at what I poured out onto the paper. I wrote about what happened, my misery, and how my mother had always looked the other way. The letter revealed how much I wanted Mom to love me; how I had tried as a child to please my mother. How as a young girl I shouldered the blame for years of abuse. It was a terribly sad letter:

Dear Nancy:

This is a difficult letter for me to write. I know what Mom and Ed are doing is wrong, but what you are feeling is real, even though Mom tells you it's not. It's not your fault! Over and over you've been hurt by Ed and Mom looked the other way.

I know you have been looking for someone to listen to you, to believe you, and no one helped; they all blamed you. You believe you are bad. That's not true!

When Ed burned your hands, you knew it wasn't right, but your mom told you it was your fault, because you were bad. When Ed hit you with your skis, your mom didn't come help. She blamed you. You were never safe at home. It's not okay to be beaten, tortured and tormented. It's not okay to have to witness your brothers being hurt, to inflict injuries on yourself or on your brothers. It's not okay to participate in sadistic games.

They're wrong! Nobody, but nobody, deserves this kind of treatment; especially not you. You're not bad; you're sweet, kind and innocent.

It's okay to be angry. Your mother should not have allowed this to happen....

The letter went on, page after page—a document of pain, a diary of self-doubt, second-hand reassurances, and a cry for help and acceptance.

After Thomas read my letter, he turned to me with compassion and understanding. "That was a lonely way to grow up," he commented softly.

"I know," was all I managed to say, fighting back tears.

Even after writing the letter, I still had some trouble recognizing the severity of the abuse, the depth of the emotional assault my brothers and I endured, and the scars that remained from feeling shame and guilt for having "caused so much trouble."

Confused and feeling terrible, I left my counselor's office. All the things I didn't remember haunted me. Trying to forgive all these years, I had suppressed my anger and memories because I couldn't forgive if I acknowledged my experiences. Forgiveness helped me to have compassion, and love for my mom. However, it hadn't helped me to love and take care of myself. What if I had exaggerated the incidents out of proportion, just as Mom always said?

I felt I was looking at a patch of color that I knew was red but everyone else in my family was angry at me and called it blue. My confidence was shaken, yet I believed red was red. I had to prove that to myself, once and for all.

Every man has his own destiny; the only imperative
is to follow it, to accept it, no matter where it leads him.
                                        —Henry Miller

Finally, I did something. Like a detective looking for shreds of evidence to solve a crime, I gathered information that related to my past. I contacted several people who had been around during my childhood and asked them to tell me what they recalled about the goings-on in my household. In a meticulous and orderly fashion, I followed through until the evidence gathered was overwhelming. I had revealed bits of the puzzle. And the pieces fitted together.

It was true—red was red!

Friends, relatives, and neighbors alike recounted endless stories of abuse. One friend remembered Ed throwing Rob down the basement stairs. He had also watched in horror as Ed rubbed my brother's face in a spill on the kitchen floor, like a puppy dog being housebroken. This friend had seen the black eyes and the bruises.

An adult cousin remembered how Ed had picked up Randy and flung him against the brick fireplace.

Everyone included stories of Ed's paddle.

A neighbor, several of my childhood pals, and some of my mother's friends confessed they had been scared silly of Ed, and had avoided coming to the house. As each person contributed some detail — some act of abuse they had witnessed—the picture grew in size and color. Its wildly clashing shades painted an obscene canvas of twisted images.

"I don't know what happened to your mother," one neighbor commented. "She went off the deep end when your dad died. She's like an alcoholic when it comes to men; she chooses awful life partners. But worse than that, she hangs on to them forever. She never saw what was happening to her children."

The neighbor's friendly voice and reassuring words were like a soothing balm for me when she said, "There's nothing you can do about your mother, but it's high time you took care of yourself. Do whatever is necessary for you to be okay. Don't let your mother pull you down any longer."

I felt a load lift. This neighbor never once suggested I "help" my mother or "forgive and forget" the past. She advised self-preservation. What a relief! How remarkable! Here was someone who not only saw my predicament, but acknowledged reality—someone who needed no explanations and made no excuses.

Staying on track, I made more phone calls, and talked to other people. My probing and searching triggered additional memories. I gathered bits and pieces belonging to the past with the passion of a rare stamp collector.

It was amazing how everyone contributed to the accumulation of overwhelming evidence that spelled ABUSE in capital letters, yet none had thought of confronting the abusers at the time.

Each phone conversation included—"I remember how you.... I remember when Ed was.... Your mother...."

After my last call I hung up the telephone and cried softly.

So many knew, but nobody helped.

CHAPTER SEVEN

Mother, I Don't Forgive You

For close to eight years I had done all the "right" things in my efforts to have the normal, loving and caring relationship with my mother I so desperately wanted. I had heeded the pet phrases and pat advice spouted by the authorities from whom I sought help. I had tried to live by their recommendations. It all had sounded so simple; a child could understand it.

Stop digging.... Yesterday is dead and gone.... Try and forget.... Forgive and Forget.... Don't get worked up.... Anger corrodes.... Everybody lives with injustice at some time.... That's life!... They did the best they could.... Making mistakes is human.... Forgive! Only through forgiveness can you heal.... Forgive ... Forget ... Forgive ... Forget ... Forgive ... Forgive....

Everywhere I turned I heard the same words: "You have to forgive." They came from my family, to my counselors and the religious community alike. I saw myself as a complete and utter failure. As though my self-esteem wasn't low enough from years of abuse, try as I might, I couldn't even get forgiving right!

Browsing the shelves of my favorite bookstore, I came across Alice Miller's book, *Breaking Down the Wall of Silence: The Liberating Experience of Facing Painful Truth.*

As I turned the pages, I was fascinated by the author's unique approach to forgiveness as the universal answer for health and healing. I couldn't put the book down. I read:

> In recent years I have been sent many books ... describing different kinds of therapeutic intervention. Without a single exception, all these authors presume that forgiveness is a condition for "successful" therapy. This notion appears to be so widespread in therapeutic circles that it is never called into question—something urgently needed. For forgiveness does not resolve latent hatred and self-hatred but rather covers them up in a very dangerous way.

The author went on to say that therapists allow themselves to be guided by their own fear and by the hope that good behavior might one day buy the love their parents denied them. The book questions the value of forgiving when parents refuse to admit to their wrong doings.

> What is constantly repeated to patients—until they believe it, and the therapist is mollified—is: "Your hate is making you ill. You must forgive and forget. Then you will be well." But it was not hatred that drove patients to mute desperation in their childhood, by alienating them from their feelings and their needs. It was such morality with which they were constantly pressured.

Alice Miller is so right! My forgiveness had not solved my latent hatred or self-hatred. She was also correct that I was guided by my fear and my hope that my good behavior would buy my mother's love. It hadn't.

Down inside, I always rebelled against the act of forgiving—erasing the past and acting like nothing had happened.

Mom's acts were indeed inexcusable. The emotions and confusions that haunted and tortured me were in direct opposition of forgiveness. But I felt the societal pressure to be a "good" person and forgive-and-forget.

I got myself ready for another visit with Thomas. While I busied myself with the house and chores, I reviewed in my mind the information and confirmations that had been the result of my detective work. I drove off to meet my therapist. Excited, I had proof that red was really red. I couldn't wait to see him and waited impatiently in his outer office. Finally, he was ready for me.

I dropped into the comfortable chair and, with a big smile in my eyes, faced my therapist. "Guess, what?" the words rushed out of me, "I've got the proof. I was right all this time. I called everyone I could remember from my childhood who might have seen or heard something and remembered. And they all came through," I ended triumphantly.

Thomas complemented me. "When you want something, you certainly go after it," he commented with a wide grin.

I confessed that I had been terribly shaken when I left him after my last session with him.

"I had to find out," I said. "I'm always so scared to get bashed over the head for talking about the past. I have consistently been punished for it before. Even now, taking to you, a part of me is still afraid you'll say it was my fault." I took a deep breath and sat back in my chair, expectantly.

"I know," was Thomas's simple reply.

Excitedly, I told him what I had learned from my friends and neighbors. As I brought details of my friends' stories out into the open, there was a note of sadness in my voice. I was awed by what I repeated to Thomas, as though something new and overwhelming had been added to my life.

"I'm so very angry at my mother!" I looked squarely at him. "Everyone tells me that I should forgive her. But how can I forgive someone who has never asked to be forgiven; somebody who's never even acknowledged any wrongdoing, someone who continues to do the same thing?"

Thomas shifted in his chair and leaned forward, resting his arms on the big, uncluttered desk in front of him. He picked up a pen, twirled it in his hand, and looked at it thoughtfully, as though the answer was hidden behind its shiny casing. He looked up at me.

"Well," he said with a sigh, "psychology for years used to counsel to forgive. But we are beginning to recognize that it isn't always possible or even healthy to do that. I believe that sometimes it is important not to forgive, and to hang onto a healthy sort of rage at what happened," he concluded, looking at me quizzically. He pulled his arms back on his lap and slowly leaned back in his chair. His eyes never left my face.

Relief, warm and feathery, washed over me and spread soothingly into every cell of my body, leaving behind a tingling sensation that bragged of being alive and whole. I would be whole again! Someone, an enlightened witness— as Alice Miller calls that someone—had listened, had understood, and had given me permission to be angry and not to forgive.

What an incredible feeling it was! There was a potent healing power in that moment, a feeling of freedom—freedom from spending every ounce of my energy trying to suppress the dam of pain. I could let the dam "wash away" and be free to experience my suffering with a full range of emotions. I could tell instantly that I'd be able to heal. I bathed in the light of self-preservation. My journey to wholeness had begun.

> *A single event can awaken within us*
> *a stranger totally unknown to us.*
> —Antoine de Saint Exupery

My eyes wavered between tears and laughter. My face lit up and smiled, surely touched by an inner source of light. I let out a deep, swooshing sigh.

"You know," I said slowly, shaking my head, "I feel more at peace with being angry than practicing forgiveness. That never was an honest emotion for me. It was always someone else's concept of what I should do. I am angry at my mother, and I also love her. I'm angry, but I don't wish her ill."

I told Thomas about a recent fight I had with my mom that had ended in my resolution to take another step toward being true to myself.

"I haven't even told you yet," I started a bit hesitatingly. "I decided not to see my mother any more. Would it be okay not to see her any more, at all?" I looked at him, not knowing what to expect.

"I believe that you should do whatever it takes to be okay. You do whatever is right for you," he replied.

"My family will be furious with me," I shuddered.

"If the whole family is mad at you, tell them I gave you permission. Let them be mad at me," Thomas stated matter-of-factly.

I burst out laughing—a joyful, bubbling sound that bounced happily into the stillness of the room, and finally brought tears of mirth to my eyes. "You know," I said, "to the adult Nancy that sounds so funny. But," I added, settling back comfortably, "there's that little girl who waited twenty-five years for someone to acknowledge that what happened really happened. That little girl has been waiting for someone to lift that awful burden from her."

To the little girl it wasn't funny. She felt wistful and a bit sad that it had taken so long to be free of being responsible for the happiness of others, free of guilt, and free not to forgive—and free to choose not to even see her mother.

"What if I never want to see my mother again?" I challenged Thomas.

"We'll have to explore that," he nodded his head. "I don't know yet if that would necessarily be the best thing for you."

I remained quiet. The very thought of having to see my mother again was overwhelming. It didn't feel good. It felt destructive, almost repulsive—like undoing all the good that was beginning to grow out of the shambles of the past for me. Mom had not changed, and throughout the years she had continued to be careless with my feelings and remained oblivious of her own contributions to my misery. There was no need for me to go back for more. I couldn't "fix" it. I had tried that in vain.

*God, grant me the serenity to accept the things I cannot
change, the courage to change the things I can,
and the wisdom to know the difference.*
—Reinhold Niebuhr

* * * * *

A few weeks later, I was relieved to have my feelings validated after reading Dr. Susan Forward's Book, *Toxic Parents: Overcoming Their Hurtful Legacy and Reclaiming Your Life*, which had made a considerable splash at New York's bestseller market.

Dr. Forward answers the question ... shouldn't I forgive my parents? with a resounding "NO!"

"This may shock, anger, dismay, or confuse you," Dr. Forward goes on to say, " In fact it is not necessary to forgive your parents in order to feel better about yourself and to change your life."

Dr. Forward, an internationally recognized therapist and author of several books, is aware that this statement flies in the face of some of our most cherished religious, spiritual, philosophical and psychological principles. According to Judeo-Christian ethics, to err is human, to forgive divine. She disagrees completely that forgiveness is not only the first step but ... the only step necessary for inner peace.

In the beginning stages of her practice, she too, believed forgiveness to be an important part of the healing process. Clients who entered her therapy sessions often stated that they had already forgiven their toxic parents, but she became aware that in spite of the saintly act, her clients didn't feel any better for having forgiven. They still felt bad about themselves.

Dr. Forward confessed that she took a long, hard look at the concept of forgiveness. "I began to wonder," she said, "if it could actually impede progress rather than enhance it." She goes on to say that there is something wrong with unquestioningly absolving someone of his rightful responsibility, particularly if he had mistreated an innocent child.

"Why in the world should you 'pardon' a father who terrorized and battered you, who made your childhood a living hell? How are you supposed to 'overlook' the fact that you had to come home to a dark house and nurse your drunken mother almost every day? And do you really have to 'forgive' a father who raped you at the age of seven?

"The more I thought about it, the more I realized that this absolution was really another form of denial. 'If I forgive you, we can pretend that what happened wasn't so terrible.'" She concluded, "I came to realize that this aspect of forgiveness was actually preventing a lot of people from getting on with their lives."

Subconsciously, I had for years wrestled with what Dr. Forward put so simply as she cleared away the cobwebs of the belief that forgiveness is the first step to healing from abuse. I agreed completely with her statement, "One of the most dangerous things about forgiveness is that it undercuts your ability to let go of your pent-up emotions. How can you acknowledge your anger against a parent whom you've already forgiven?"

Dr. Forward was the next person after Thomas who humanized the act of unforgiving and made it respectable.

Once I was able to set aside the notion of forgiving, at least for the present, it opened the door for me to seriously examine the past without any limits and to fit the pieces to the puzzle that kept me from healing myself. I knew I was missing something buried in my subconscious, something awful that Ed did. If only I could remember what it was, I would be able to feel.

The next session with Thomas would be one of the most revealing and healing moments I experienced—which set me on the path to capturing a full life as a whole human being.

CHAPTER EIGHT

My Father's Eyes

Forgiveness is not a commodity that can be handed out.
It is a relationship that must be entered into.
— Karl Rahner

It was a true Northwest winter day. The weather was cool and rainy when I left the house to keep my appointment with Thomas.

At my counselor's office, I draped my raincoat over the hat rack, parked my umbrella, and walked into Thomas's comfortable room. "Good to see you," was the mutual friendly greeting as we settled into our familiar chairs. I was eager to get this session going. This was the day to explore guided imagery. Thomas explained guided imagery to me at my insistence. I had to recall what my mind had so well hidden. I knew that it meant going back to view myself at another time and another age, simply for the clarification and validation of the actual happenings. Thomas, the therapist, would guide me through the maze of vague and never-remembered-before memories.

"I want you to relax," said Thomas, "close your eyes—relax! Ignore anything that doesn't fit and don't accept anything that's uncomfortable."

I leaned into my chair, closed my eyes, and drifted back.

"How old are you, Nancy?" Thomas asked in a quiet voice.

"Eight," came my laconic reply.

"Can you see yourself?"

"Yes."

"Describe yourself."

"My hair is short; my eyes are big and bright."

"What are you doing?"

"I'm singing."

"What are you singing?"

"*You are my sunshine.*"

"Do you feel safe?"

"Yes."

"Now, move forward to a time when you're not safe," Thomas directed me.

"How old are you?"

"Nine."

"Can you tell me what's happening? Why you're not safe?"

"No."

"Why not?"

"Because there's a big brick wall there."

"Okay; what if we try to remove the wall?"

My chest tightened and my body ached. I felt that I needed the wall for my survival.

"What if you'd imagine a waterfall washing away the wall?"

I could see that brick wall—strong, solid. I saw water rushing over it. I relaxed when I realized the wall wouldn't budge. The waterfall couldn't wash it away.

"No! It won't wash away."

"What if you had some protection first? If you had a suit of armor, would the wall go away?"

"No."

"How about a big brute of a guy to protect you?"

"No. I still wouldn't feel safe."

"Can you think of anything that would protect you?"

"My father's eyes."

"Can you see his eyes?"

"Yes."

"What do they look like?"

"They look like they adore me."

"Are you and your father touching?"

"No."

"Can you still see his eyes?"

"Yes."

I started to cry softly. I felt so safe; I didn't know why I was crying.

"Can Ed get there? Can he get to where you and your father are?"

"Yes," I shuddered.

"Can you take your father somewhere else, a place where people can't go unless you invite them?"

"Yes."

"Are you there?"

"Yes."

"Can you see his eyes?"

"Yes."

"Is there anything you want to tell your father?"

"I want to tell him that I don't want him to die."

"Do you want to tell him what happened after he died?"

"I can't think of what to tell him."

"Do you have a special place on yourself where you can tuck him away?"

"Yes."

"Whenever you need him, you can touch that special place, and he will be there for you. Now, I want you to spend a moment with your father. Take all the time you need. When you're ready, say good-bye to him and open your eyes."

I felt the familiar tightness rise in my chest. I didn't want to say good-bye. I waited a few moments, said good-bye to my father, and opened my eyes.

That was the only guided imagery session I had. It was the only one I ever needed. Although the session failed to reveal what I was looking for, I left Thomas in a more peaceful and quiet mood than ever before.

A few days later, I had a dream about visiting with my father. He looked well and appeared to be quite young. His face was fuller than I remembered. But he was so big, his image so real, that I was almost sure it wasn't a dream at all.

There we were, father and daughter, face to face as adults. My eyes brimmed over. I told my father I was crying because I was so happy to see him. He didn't know he had died.

As the dream continued, my mother and the boys walked in. A few more scenes played on, and I wanted to tell my father something important. But Mom and the boys looked at me in anger, and I woke up in a cold sweat. I was frightened and at the same time cross for waking before I heard what I was about to tell my father. I was frustrated because I knew it was the missing link.

Eventually I knew what it was. I realized that every time I confided in someone about the incidents of abuse at home, Mom got into the act and tried to destroy my relationship with that person. She would depict me as the unbalanced, problematic troublemaker, the most difficult of all her children. That was the worst abuse of all. I was betrayed by my mother. I was all alone in a very scary world—without anyone in my corner. Perhaps I wasn't going to tell my father. I was plain scared of telling anyone. Had I told him, Mom would have found a way to discredit me and he, too, would have been angry at me. I couldn't risk that. I couldn't afford to lose that one and only perfect relationship from my childhood. That's why the dream ended.

I sat up in bed, took a deep breath, touched that special place, and my father was with me. I looked into his adoring eyes. I was safe. I didn't have to tell him about the abuse. I didn't have to present proof that I was the victim and not the criminal and that I deserved to be loved. His eyes filled with sadness.

He already knew. What a wonderful feeling. He already knew.

* * * * *

My relationship with my mother and consequently, with Brandon dried up like a weed at the end of summer. I didn't speak to Mom, nor would I have anything to do with Smokey, who continued to abuse Brandon. Mom, in turn, forbade Brandon to see me, or talk to me. Rob had long stopped any kind of contact with me and had placed his blind loyalty with his mother. Smokey continued to rule the roost, and his behavior was as despicable as ever.

There was one more occasion in which I spoke to my mother. I called her on Brandon's behalf, but instead of coming to some sort of a resolution for his sake, I listened as Mom ranted about how I had destroyed the family, that I was sick, a crybaby, and a crazy troublemaker. When she completed her tirade, she hung up on me. Although the entire family steadfastly maintained that I was sick, I don't believe they really thought that I was ill. They never tried to help me with my "illness," nor did they tell me which mental disorder they believed I had.

After numerous confrontations with my mother on the subject of past and present abuse, I realized that if she hadn't done anything about it in twenty-five years, she wasn't about to acknowledge it now.

I decided it was time to divorce my mother. I realized that in order to continue my recovery process, I would not be able to see her or Rob. It was a difficult decision, since I still loved her and felt for her pain. I also knew that the biggest contribution for healing could have come from Mom. I understood that it would never be and that I had to work on my recovery by myself. Mom and Rob had always robbed me of any progress I experienced.

The most important piece of the puzzle finally emerged. I had been too frightened to see it before. I recalled clearly the acts of torture Ed had inflicted. But that wasn't it. I wasn't afraid of those memories.

"I am aware that it was my mother who had caused the irreparable damage." I sat up straight and looked at Thomas. "It wasn't her striking me that hurt the most," I continued breathlessly. "She slapped me and spanked me; she used the paddle on me and yanked me by my hair. But it is the chilling fact she didn't protect me and what she said to me that hurt the most.

"I feel so betrayed by my mother. Our family unit can not survive without my role as the scapegoat. The exclusion is unbearable.

"She had called me a fucking bitch, continually accused me of being sick and a crazy troublemaker. There is an emotional pain so severe, one cannot bear it, or live with it. It threatens your very survival.

"Every time my mother acted in an emotionally abusive manner, to me or to someone I loved, no matter what the intensity of the abuse, it triggered a subconscious recall of a time in my young life when I felt so trapped and at her mercy that my death seemed like the only way to stop the intolerable pain.

"Each abusive encounter felt like it threatened my very existence. And even though I believe that the family members made their own choices about shutting me out, they must have been somewhat influenced by her accusations." I paused for a moment before I continued.

"And she left me unprotected as a child. I was vulnerable and at the mercy of the sadist she married and brought into my life. I survived a lot. I am lucky to be alive. It is remarkable I didn't abuse my children."

I let myself sink slowly back into my chair and added softly, "I know that my emotional survival hinges on staying away from my mother."

As I continued to read books on self-development in my search for material on the subject of abuse, I came across Beverly Engels' book, *Divorcing a Parent*, subtitled: *Free Yourself from the Past and Live the Life You've Always Wanted*.

The book caught my eye, not only because I had decided to divorce my own mother, but because it was endorsed by Dr. Harold H. Bloomfield, author of *Making Peace with Your Parents*. He acknowledged that sometimes, in cases of abuse, peace wasn't possible.

Each page I turned fortified the knowledge that I had made the right choice. For the first time in twenty-five years, I was comfortable. The message in the book validated my choice for healing: "I can't forgive you, Mother." That had to be it—for now, maybe even forever.

There was neither malice nor revenge in my actions. If anything, there was a lot of sadness and a grieving for the loss of a young girl's dreams. I mourned the loss of the mother she "could have been," and buried beneath that loss was the love that I felt for her.

Most therapists have come to the conclusion that no matter how abusive a parent is—children will most probably always love their mother.

"I wish there was some way I could divorce my mother" is the first line in Engels' book as she recounts one of her patient's wishful pleadings for permission to separate herself from an abusive parent.

"Even if I could forgive her for the past," the young woman said to the author, "I can't keep forgiving her for hurting me over and over again. There's got to be a time when forgiveness ceases and self-preservation takes over. How can I continue to recover if she continually undermines my self-esteem? I really wish I never had to see her again."

Engels writes that many of her clients confess they wish they didn't have to deal with their parents any more. Every one of the people who sought her counsel was either physically, emotionally, and/or sexually abused.

Engels, in agreement with Dr. Forward, states that until recently (circa 1990) the idea of divorcing a parent was not a popular one, and that most therapists encouraged their clients to have sympathy for their parents and to learn to forgive them for their mistakes.

There are several fine books on the market, Engels observes, that advocate getting along with one's parents. There is Dr. Harold H. Bloomfield's *Making Peace with Your Parents*: and *My Mother, Myself*, by Nancy Friday. Notable among other works is Howard Halpern's *Cutting Loose: An Adult Guide to Coming to Terms with Your Parents*.

"But as wise as all these therapists, books and philosophies are," Engels continues, "forgiveness is difficult and sometimes impossible. In reality, there are thousands of people who, no matter how hard they have tried to understand their parents, cannot forgive them."

Engels further comments that, "The notion of divorcing a parent is taboo in our society."

The author goes on to explain the expectations conveyed to the adult child to make never-ending compromises and confirms my experiences with my own mother. No matter how cruel my mom was or how unchanging she continued to be, the responsibility for change and forgiveness always fell on me. According to Engels', this experience was consistent with those she had seen in her practice.

I read every word in these books and found immense relief in the fact that each paragraph so accurately described and validated my thoughts and feelings. Page after page brought me the strange feeling that I was reading my own life story. Someone had put down on paper exactly what I had experienced, how I felt, what I faced, and what I had feared. And, above all, that there was an alternative available.

I read with fascination how Engels agreed that another very important factor of forgiving comes to us straight from the teachings of the Christian ideology. Jesus forgave us our sins, and God taught us forgiveness. For the many who embrace these principles and apply them to every inch of their lives, not to forgive, especially a parent (honor thy mother and father), is just not acceptable. At the same time they remain upset, deal from anger, and are far from being healed.

In my on-going search for material on the subject, I came across an article by Richard Lord in *The Christian Century* magazine titled, "*Do I Have to Forgive?*"* which describes the minister's search for answers to "forgiveness" for one of his parishioners. He has come up with some astonishing and provocative thoughts.

"What can we learn from the Judeo-Christian tradition about forgiveness which does not imply forgetting or excusing? On Yom Kippur, sins against God are forgiven. But if you have sinned against your neighbor, you must go to him or her and seek forgiveness. Not even God forgives you what you have done to another. This perspective is dramatically present in Simon Wiesenthal's *The Sunflower*.

*Copyright 1991 *Christian Century*. Reprinted with permission from the October 9, 1991, issue of the *Christian Century*. P. 902

Wiesenthal, a Jew in a Nazi concentration camp, is led to the bedside of a dying German soldier. The soldier confesses that he took part in the killing of Jews and wants Wiesenthal to forgive him before he dies.

Unable to do so, Wiesenthal turns and leaves the young man's side. He believes he has no right to forgive the soldier for what he did to other people. He imagines meeting dead Jews in Heaven and hearing them ask: 'Who gave you the right to forgive our murder?'"

The minister added that he no longer says in a general public way, "Your sins are forgiven."

The article goes on to say, "Dietrich Bonhoeffer wrote that 'cheap grace is the preaching of forgiveness without requiring repentance.' Repentance has traditionally involved three aspects which guard against cheap grace: remorse, restitution and regeneration. First, a genuine 'Sorry' is required. Second, insofar as possible, an attempt must be made to restore what was destroyed. This means accepting legal, financial and moral consequences. Third, there must be a renewal, a change in how the person lives. 'Fruits of repentance' should show evidence that the sin will not be repeated.

"This threefold character is seen in one of the invitations to Holy Communion. 'You that do ... truly and earnestly repent of your sins; and are in love and charity with your neighbor; and intend to live a new life ...'

"To offer forgiveness when these conditions are not met is not gracious. It is sacrilegious. Forgiveness is not a commodity that can be handed out. It is a relationship that must be entered into."

CHAPTER NINE

Setting the Foundation

It is my pleasure that my children are free,
happy and unrestrained by parental tyranny.
Love is the chain whereby to bind a child to its parents.
—Abraham Lincoln

The next time I saw Thomas, I settled into my accustomed chair and told him about the great weekend I had spent with the girls. I was wistful as I recalled some of the funny things they said and reiterated just how much I appreciated them.

Thomas smiled, but before he could say a thing, I looked him straight in the eyes and announced, "Thomas, I've decided to divorce my mother!"

Words rushed out of me at top speed, and my voice rang with both exhilaration and sadness, as I told him about the book I had read, *Divorcing a Parent*, which confirmed my earlier decision not to see my mother anymore.

"I discovered that I had already gone through many of the emotional steps the author mentioned. I know that my mother is both good and bad, but the bad overshadows the good. It's all I'm ever offered and I can't live with it any longer.

"Are you shutting out the possibility of ever seeing her again?"

"No, not exactly," I spoke slowly now, thoughtfully weighing my words.

"For the sake of saving myself, and my sanity, it is my intention to divorce her forever, even if she falls ill. I feel comfortable with my decision. I have been through enough, and the wear and tear of trying to have even a casual relationship with her is killing me. I do miss her. I love her, that's what makes it so sad. However, I don't believe she loves me, nor do I think she will ever change, and I won't seek a reconciliation myself," I concluded, my voice strong and clear.

"She would have to stop what's happening to Brandon," I continued, "and she would have to make amends. Only then would I consider the possibility of forgiving her. But until that happens," I paused with my eyes locked on Thomas's face, "I can't let her hurt me again. My pain it too great. I can't forgive her. And, that goes for Rob as well. I have to divorce him too."

Thomas nodded in silent agreement.

"I found a great section in Beverly Engels' book *Divorcing a Parent*," I announced triumphantly pointing to the cover. "Her work confirms my experiences with my brothers.

"Robs' behavior towards me has been confusing; however, according to Engels, my experiences with my brother are very common. She explains that siblings are often the least supportive of anyone because even though the same parent has also damaged them, they are often in so much denial that they are threatened by your attempts to recover. They can't listen to what your parent has done to you, because they are unable to face what their parent has done to them.

"Let me read you just one short paragraph. It was written for me! It fits my situation with Rob to a T," I smiled.

I opened the book, which had been flagged with a dozen blue stickers marking the places that were so familiar and pertinent to me.

Thomas settled back in his chair and listened attentively as I started to read. I opened the book at a place I had marked and read from a section called, "When Siblings View You as the Enemy":

"Usually there is one child in a family who seems to be the one to stand up and confront the abuse.... Siblings often accuse this person of being disloyal to the parent, of making trouble, or refusing to let bygones be bygones, and of constantly harping about the past. They may see her as the crazy, neurotic, or troubled one—yet, ironically, this child is often the healthiest and strongest of all."

I closed the book and looked up at Thomas. He nodded his head several times, a light smile across his lips, "That leaves you Randy. It would be nice if you could save one relationship from your family of origin."

"He's coming to visit next week, and I can bring him in if that's okay," I questioned.

In his usual manner, Thomas replied, "Whatever you need is okay with me."

I found the validation I had craved in books and in therapy. Because I hadn't yet received validation in the real world, these professionals became my oasis.

Contrary to popular belief, healing required stepping out of my relationships, out of the desire to forgive and to become "selfish," focusing only on myself and on what I needed.

Although research and therapy were imperative to set the foundation for healing, it was time to take the next step and build on this foundation in the real world. I couldn't fully heal until I risked expressing my needs to others.

In the ensuing years, I often found myself thrust back to my foundation with an uncompromising resolve to put myself first in this process no matter what losses putting myself first required.

As soon as I arrived at home, I called Randy, and a strange and convoluted conversation took place. When I hung up the phone, I walked into the living room, curled up in the corner of the couch, rested my head against the softness of the upholstery, closed my eyes, and ran over the talk I had with my younger brother, just to see if I'd missed something.

I had explained to Randy things we had discussed before, my decision to divorce myself from mom. I assured him that all I wanted from him was a continued relationship.

"I know what goes on in this family," he replied, "but I live in California, and what little I see of my family is important to me. It's my family! I really would like us to be able to talk with each other without digging around in all the "bad" stuff. Let's talk about good things."

I quickly picked up my end and said, "Look, Randy, I'd like us to have a fun, normal relationship. One that is also understanding and supportive. However, I won't deny reality. I'll not forget who I am, where I came from, and what happened. I'll never accept the abuse we all experienced, and I don't want to be dragged back into it either."

I received a telephone call from Randy at Thanksgiving. We chatted amicably for a while, but our conversation stayed safely in the trivia category.

He decided not to see me any more, and simply walked out of my life.

His loss saddened me the most.

CHAPTER TEN

Mourning

When it is all said and done ...
I cannot change other people; they walk their own path,
And they live by what they perceive to be the truth.
Only by changing my perception and awareness
Can I change my circumstance.
—the author

Even though my relationship with Mom, Rob and Randy had been more than rocky and unstable for a long time, I still missed them. I never told Mom and Rob of my decision to stop seeing them. Nor did they question me about my disappearance. We simply never spoke again. I consider myself a real "family" person, and the separation from my mother and brothers has created a void. During the years I have become very close to Aunt Julie, my mother's sister, and have found in her a true and valuable friend.

My grandparents were the only other family members with whom I kept in touch regularly. I visited them once a week and was pleased that they were in good health and able to maintain a comfortable lifestyle.

But even my relationship with them came to an abrupt end one day, and I had to call on all of my reserves and inner resources to live with it. The break came when I casually mentioned to my grandmother that I was still plodding along working on my manuscript. Grandma came apart.

"I don't think you should continue with this book of yours. Why don't you just leave it alone? You will live to regret it," she said crossly. "I've held my tongue as long as I could. I told you ten years ago you should not say bad things about your mother. I don't believe the things you talk about happened. I don't believe it was that bad."

She continued her attack, accusing me of having been a difficult and incorrigible child. All of a sudden, she recalled a list of incidents from my adolescence, viewing normal teenage behavior as uncontrollable.

"Your mother did the best she could!" Grandmother shouted, "But you were always causing trouble, always rebelling against her, and you did what you wanted!"

Grandpa pleaded with Grandma, "Stop it Opal! Stop it. Nancy was a wonderful child."

Grandma ignored his pleas and said as she left the room, "I'm disgusted with you, and I suppose this is the end of our friendship."

Stunned and shocked, I let the onslaught of insults cascade over me. I followed her to the kitchen and tried to negotiate a relationship with her, setting up boundaries that would exclude mentioning Mom and the manuscript I was in the process of completing. However, Grandma made it clear that it wasn't possible, and I ended my visit with a quiet, "I love you."

I collected my children, grabbed my purse, and left the house forever that so long had been more than a home to me. I helped the girls into the car, opened the door to the driver's side, straightened my shoulders, and looked back at my grandparents' home for the last time. My grandmother, like all people, had made her own choice. She clung to a different reality, one I couldn't change.

I went home and cried all day. I recalled the weekly visits at my grandparents' house, the genuine exchange of love and camaraderie, the shared laughter and the sense of family that would be no more. Sadly, I mourned another loss.

> *We shall draw from the heart of suffering itself,*
> *the means of inspiration and survival.*
> —Sir Winston Churchill

I had lived my life "on edge," worried that my mother, grandmother, and brothers didn't love me just as I was, but rather only if I behaved just as they wanted. I was devastated that my fears were correct.

Having lost every relationship from my family of origin, I realized it was necessary to build a completely new life for myself. It took years of hard work to formulate healthy relationships and new family traditions for my daughters and myself.

The first holidays were particularly difficult; however, after a few years, our new holiday traditions were more loving and meaningful than any of my prior experiences.

My friends have become a fortress of love, understanding and support for me. They gathered around me and showered me with affection and caring. They touched my heart in ways my family never did and showed me the true rewards of recovery.

I am so grateful for my Aunt Julie, my cousins and our ever-deepening relationships. It is a wonderful feeling to walk into my aunt's house and feel love in the room.

When I stopped seeing Thomas, he told me that I would be "recovering" for the rest of my life. I didn't believe him; at least I did not want to. However, after years of experience, I now understand that we can process only so much pain at once.

Initially, the love I felt from my extended family and friends seemed satisfying; nevertheless, as I moved on with my life, the private affection I received was not enough to help me move through my recovery. Again, I found myself suffering in silence.

I strongly believe that this kind of abuse simply cannot heal unless our injuries are acknowledged in a public way.

Often I have witnessed humanity's disbelief when a relative forgives a loved one's murder. "How can you forgive murder?" is our collective outcry.

I have come to understand that forgiveness is not necessarily predicated on the degree of the offence but rather on the justice we receive. In other words—did the murderer go to trial? Did the community acknowledge the offence?

I have found that, in general, those who forgive crimes of violence have seen some sort of justice. Not revenge. Simply justice.

For victims of childhood violence, receiving justice is often not the case. Rarely do child abusers see the inside of a courtroom and rarer still do they admit their offences.

How do we forgive something that in the eyes of our community did not happen?

Unfortunately, my extended family and a number of my friends over-lapped with that of my family of origin. Therefore, the negative comments Mom, Rob, Randy and Grandma spoke about me, were repeated to me often. Although we lived completely separate lives, I still heard their voices:

- I was sick.
- I was a troublemaker.
- I single-handedly destroyed the family.
- I should be nice to my mother.

Even though I had the private support of many people—I did not have anyone's public support. The truth was—the abuse in our family caused a major fracture, and unless that abuse was addressed, the fracture could not be mended. Publicly—nobody confronted my family with this.

As I said before, people have trouble confronting abuse. The natural tendency is to avoid confrontation and unpleasantness; therefore, I stood alone.

My family's assessment of me was met with silence. At worst, others accepted I was to blame for the family fracture—at best, others expressed that everyone should mind their own business and have their own relationships.

Because speaking about the abuse had resulted in the loss of my entire family of origin, it would be many years before I had the courage to break my silence again. Finally, when the silent misery I lived with out-weighed the risk of another wave of losses—I asked for the public support of my friends and extended family.

If you know a victim or a survivor, please stand by that individual and publicly speak the truth. Nobody can stand alone; the silence is crushing. Without validation, we become "frozen" in the abuse. As survivors, we need help changing the majority voice we hear from that of our abusers—to that of love; so that we can heal, mourn, and move on with our lives.

My biggest source of pride is my children.

I rejoice that all my hard work paid off and I can celebrate with them a loving relationship. I have the opportunity to show them what it is to be a woman, a mother, and God willing, some day a grandmother. My longing for a close mother-daughter relationship has been realized with them. How fortunate we all are.

As I've shared with them all the important events and passages in their lives, I have simultaneously experienced joy and sorrow. Joy at their milestones, happy to guide, advise and protect. I brim with pride and enthusiasm for them. Then quietly, I mourn for myself. As my children grow, I've come to realize just how much I missed out on.

My lost experiences hit me without warning at Tara's high school graduation. As I sat in the arena, my eyes roamed the crowd. I beamed with pride and soaked up the joy of the moment. I reflected on my children's growing up years and all of the exciting events we had shared and celebrated—when out-of-the-blue, a feeling of complete sadness engulfed me. For the first time, I felt the impact of Mom's absence in my own growing up years. I wrestled with feelings of jealousy when I realized I hadn't received the love that I was very grateful to give to my own children.

Once again, my childhood cast a shadow on a joyous day.

Although I *knew* I didn't have the unconditional love of my mother, for the first time, I *felt* it and it felt bad.

I love my children unconditionally whether I like their behavior or not. I love them just as they are and they know it. I am grateful for the few short years I had with my father. He gave me nine years of unconditional love so that I could give it to my own children and remember the feeling for myself.

Witnessing the mother-daughter relationship in others is especially sad. Watching mothers as they share life's passages—passing on love and wisdom to their daughters. This is never so apparent to me as when I witness the closeness of mothers and daughters, where a mother guides her daughter through pregnancy, and shares the joy of childbirth.

I experienced all the important events and passages in my life without my mother by my side, something so vital to a young woman's development. There was no motherly guiding, advising, protecting and sharing of womanly matters whenever I needed it.

Carrying a baby, preparing for birth, shopping, planning, fretting, celebrating, worrying and enjoying—all the privileges grandmothers-to-be- jealously guard and want to have a hand in, I missed out on. However, when the time comes, I look forward to sharing these experiences with my own daughters.

I remembered the birth of my own girls. I was crushed at my mother's response each time David called to tell her she had a lovely new granddaughter. She was disappointed; she had wanted grandsons.

When my girls were born, Mom didn't call me in the hospital to congratulate me, nor did she visit me. In the ensuing years as the girls were growing up, she paid no more attention to them than she had in their infancy. However, when my brother had a son, she was a doting grandmother. Mom didn't celebrate my daughters' births, and come to think of it—she didn't celebrate my own.

I came across some old letters Mom and Dad wrote home to my grandparents when I was born in Germany. Dad's letters reflected the pride and joy of a new father and he thought I was beautiful. In Mom's letter the only mention of me was, "This baby is so homely—I don't think I'll be able to warm up to her."

I think she was right.

Mourning is a very long process; one that is prompted by many things.

The physical abuse my brothers and I endured during childhood and the betrayal of our mother was just the tip of the iceberg.

Years passed before I could see beyond the abuse and betrayal we all suffered, to comprehend the extent of the emotional abuse my mother reserved just for me.

In fact, since I was a child, Mom told me that although she loved me, she didn't like me. She said that she preferred boys over girls. Mom hugged and cuddled the boys, while I was the lonely, lost bystander to her show of affection. I was starved for attention, while she insisted I didn't like to be hugged.

Memories flooded back for me as I mourned increasing losses.

There was the time our family went camping when I was seven years old. Mom snapped picture after picture of Dad and the boys. When I begged her to take "just one" of me, she sent me crying to the camper, telling me the pictures were just for "Mama's men."

No matter what my brothers did or how perfectly I tried to behave—Mom physically and emotionally loved Rob and Randy and was cruel and abusive to me.

The day after Dad died, Rob at ten years old and me at nine, stayed home from school. The next morning, Mom woke me and told me to get ready for my third-grade class. When I told her that I wasn't ready to go back to school, she replied firmly, "Rob says it's time to go back—so it's time to go back!"

Each time Mom was without a man in her life, she partnered with my brother Rob and gave him her allegiance and authority.

The deprivation of Mom's love and the unhealthy balance of power in our family was a recipe for pain and loss.

Occasionally, when my hurt and frustration seemed unmanageable, I confided in my brothers the pain I felt concerning Mom's callous detachment from me. Each time I reached out for help, they became angry and banded together with Mom. Every incident brought out the painful reality that the love of my brothers was conditional on accepting Moms' cruelty.

I remained the family scapegoat. Mom and the boys belonged to a club that could never include me.

As adults, Rob and Randy were willing to look past Mom's betrayal of us as children because she held them in high esteem.

I was angry with my brothers for abandoning me. Unable to enjoy a relationship with Rob and Randy independent of my mother, left me feeling hurt and betrayed. I loved my brothers very much. I fondly recalled the fun we

had together as very young children and the bond we
shared apart from the adults in our lives. Our only major
disagreements concerned Mom and abuse.

I don't reserve sadness just for myself; I also feel very
sad for my brothers, because I love them and I know that
they love me too. I believe that they would like to have a
relationship with me; however, I don't believe they know
how. Fifty percent of the solution to any problem lies in
identifying the problem. As long as my brothers misidentify
the cause of our family fracture as my "illness," we are
unable to mend the actual cause of our fracture. Sadly, I
think we all suffer from the brokenness of our family.

The loss of my father was compounded by the loss of
his sentimental legacy. I was excluded from sharing in the
family heirlooms. Mom honored all Dads' promises to my
brothers; however, once again she banned me. The exclusion from Dads legacy was never as evident as it was when
Mom transferred the lake property Dad purchased before
their marriage and that we all loved so dearly, to "Mama's
men"; Rob, Randy, and my half-brother Brandon.

Mom talked to her friends about her sons with pride
while she told them that I was a bitch.

The ongoing difficulties I experience with my mother
were more about the way she treated me than about what
her husbands did. Mom's treatment of her only daughter
was a huge form of abuse my brothers didn't receive and
refused to understand.

After many years of uncovering deeper and deeper
layers of pain and loss, I realized my exclusion from the
family didn't have anything to do with the physical abuse
we all sustained or with taking a stand as "the trouble-

maker"—it had to do with the lifelong lonely position I held as the daughter that wasn't loved by her mother.

The most difficult pain for me to free myself from, was knowing that my mother loved my brothers, but she didn't love me.

From Hope Edelman's book, *Motherless Daughters: The Legacy of Loss,* come the words that so succinctly describe my feelings to this day: "Our mothers are our most direct connection to our history and our gender. Regardless of how well we think they did their job, the void their absence creates in our lives is never completely filled again."

It had been so hard for me to let go of my mother, however, as I mourned her loss, I realized our relationship didn't really come to an end; it never really started.

CHAPTER ELEVEN

Forgiveness
Is a Process

The soul cannot forgive until it is restored to wholeness
and health. In the absence of love—how can one forgive?
With an abundance of love, starting with one's self,
forgiveness becomes a viable opportunity.
—the author

For two years, I worked obsessively to achieve publication of my manuscript titled, *Mother I Don't Forgive You: A Necessary Alternative for Healing.* My disappointment was palpable when my dream failed to come to fruition. I surrendered my quest for publication and abandoned my manuscript.

After a four-year separation from my family, I remained clear about my feelings towards my mother. Occasionally, I had a good recollection about her, and I felt the warmth of that memory. Other times, I had a bad recollection and experienced again the darkness of that time. However, each memory stood alone. I accepted each retrospection singularly for what it was, good or bad, without judging my mother in a general way. This isn't to say that sometimes anger didn't creep in, it did. And so did sadness. Even today.

Years passed before it dawned on me that I could not think of anything that would keep me from my own daughters. The depth of my sadness reverberated through my being when I realized that if one of my children stopped seeing me, I'd move heaven and earth to restore our relationship. How incredibly sad that my mother unquestioningly allowed one of her children to simply walk away. Although I never felt loved by my mother, the reality of my situation hit hard.

Now and again, I revisited my feelings. How would I feel if my mother died? How would I feel if she were ill? My feelings had not changed. Although I definitely did not wish her harm, I shuddered at the thought of seeing her again under any circumstances. However, my hope for her was to find only happiness in every aspect of her life.

Towards my grandmother, I felt quite differently. My grandparents meant a great deal to me. I cherished fond memories of them and endured deep sadness at not being able to see them. I wished my grandmother was merely my grandmother, rather than depriving me of her company for simply telling the truth. My Grandfather was suffering the onset of Alzheimer's disease and didn't remember what had happened, or why I was gone. I fervently wished I could see him. When I checked my feelings on Grandma, I was torn. I had not fully mourned her loss. Nonetheless, when my grandmother fell ill, I could not risk any further emotional persecution. I did not go see her.

Shortly after she had recovered from her illness, I decided to take the risk of re-establishing this important relationship. In the form of a letter, I told her I loved her and missed her. I expressed my desire to see her, hoping we could find a way of being together without talking about my mother.

Grandma never answered my letter, but my younger brother Brandon, then eighteen, did write a response. My excitement was obvious when I pulled the envelope from the mailbox. Surprise and disappointment quickly replaced my enthusiasm as I read the contents of his letter.

Brandon's message was a testimonial to hate, fear and anger—all directed at me. He blamed me for tearing our family apart, and for the permanent scars my unforgivable acts have left on our family. He lamented at how I could hurt my grandparents writing such a "callous" letter. He wished me ill and condemned me to a life of loneliness.

Brandon and I had always enjoyed a loving relationship. When my mother forbade him to see me, I assumed we would see each other again when he had grown up and made his own decisions.

Originally, my brother's letter was nothing more than a reminder of why I did not see my family. However, one thought remained with me. Brandon was unaware of what he had done. Even though his actions were intentional, I did understand him. I was certain this young man with whom I previously only had loving contact, did not know what he was doing. He made judgments without understanding all the facts.

This concept began to gnaw at me. I wrestled with the meaning of forgiveness and why I could clearly feel so UN-forgiving towards my family, yet have a sense of peace and understanding towards Brandon's actions. The two feelings seemed incongruent. Often, when I shared my story with others, they said, "I think you have forgiven your mother."

For a long time I thought people said that to me because they had a hard time with the concept of non-forgiveness. Clearly, in my mind I did not forgive or I would be able to see my mother. Forgiveness is a very complicated concept. It requires exploration and growth.

In the quiet of my home, I sorted through my beliefs, shaken at the possibility that I may have overlooked something. I didn't take the "traditional path of forgiveness." Instead, I spent many years comfortable without forgiving. I found validation in both Christian and psychological books and articles and bathed in the light of my recovery.

I began to wonder if there were more.

What if there was a "non-traditional path to forgiveness" that didn't require accepting or excusing abusive behavior and I was only partially through the process?

I entertained the possibility that after healing steps are taken, and we are liberated from our abuse, we are set free to forgive.

In *Breaking Down the Wall of Silence*, Alice Miller makes a powerful statement (referring to her own therapy) when she says, "it was precisely the opposite of forgiveness—namely, rebellion against mistreatment suffered, the recognition and condemnation of my parents' destructive opinions and actions, and the articulation of my own needs—that ultimately freed me from the past."

Miller, along with Dr. Susan Forward, author of *Toxic Parents*, Beverly Engels who wrote *Divorcing a Parent*, and numerous other authorities as well as a seemingly endless string of survivors, all agree that no one should have to endure unhealthy relationships that threaten their well-

Heal and Forgive

being, and that the traditional path of forgiveness closes the path to freedom.

My attempts to forgive before healing had taken place were comparable to fighting against the tide. Now that an adequate amount of healing was accomplished, I found myself riding with the tide and ebbing naturally towards forgiveness as my resistance slowly washed away.

My transition didn't come quickly or easily, but over years my sense of peace grew deeper and my understanding greater.

Each day, I journeyed further down the path of recovery, realizing that the act of forgiveness is not necessarily bound to the choice of whether or not to see someone. Nor is it dependent on excusing offensive behavior. I made great strides towards forgiveness when I realized I didn't have to trust my mother enough to resume a relationship with her in order to forgive her; nor did I have to excuse what she'd done. I could forgive my mother and not see her.

We have all heard the sage wisdom, "You must forgive in order to heal." Each time I heard this popular phrase— anger and frustration rose from the depths of my emotions. I knew that the traditional "forgive and heal" advice didn't work for me. Placing forgiveness first was backwards and ineffectual. However, when I turned them around and made my focus healing, both healing and forgiving became realistic goals.

Prior to healing, a difficult forgiveness-concept to grasp is that of compassion for the offender. Any thought of the "spiritual oneness" we all share is well beyond our comprehension.

With my anger long subsided, I was ready to take the last step. I needed more—I needed the kind of love in my life that radiated into every corner of my heart and was central in my being. I knew that to achieve such a place would take a firm commitment and constant hard work.

A number of years ago I heard about an exercise a woman used in order to forgive her rapist. The survivor visualized God's loving hand tenderly embracing a heart with two separate chambers. God safely cradled the woman in one chamber while He cradled her attacker in the other. As a mother who unconditionally loves her own children, this was an easy visualization for me. I used this exercise often with my mother and myself.

At this point in my recovery, I still do not forgive my mother's actions. However, I am finally at a place where I can forgive her being. I truly love my mother. I am grateful she gave me life and I find great comfort in the "spiritual oneness" we all share. She is in my daily thoughts and in my prayers.

Evidence of forgiveness is found within the heart.

The Reverend Mary Manin Morrissey in her book, *Building Your Field of Dreams,** recounts the story of a parishioner named Julie, who was repeatedly raped and terrorized both physically and emotionally by her father. After seventeen years of no contact with her father, Julie wrote him a postcard to which he did not respond.

"The silence hurt her anew; the daughter who had been so violated by her father had actually reached out to him, and he had rebuffed her," the author writes. "Her

*Copyright © 1996 by Mary Manin Morrissey. Used by permission of Bantam Books, a division of Random House, Inc.

initial reaction was rage: 'How dare he ignore me, after all he's done!' She nursed her new hurt for a time, as any of us might, and then she returned to work. I say 'work' because forgiveness can be an arduous, challenging process, and sometimes we're tempted to skip work and stay home. Or we perform our jobs absentmindedly, our hearts not really in the task before us. Forgiveness may be the most difficult work you ever do. It also promises the greatest rewards."

"So whether or not her father responded to the postcard," Morrissey continues, "Julie needed to forgive him— not for his sake but for her own. Forgiveness was the only way she could release herself from her past. As long as she refused to forgive her father, she would feel like damaged goods.

"Forgiveness is a process. We forgive a piece at a time as we go on with our lives. Often, after we think we have finished, more pain arises from the same circumstance, and we must work through that next layer. Each time we become that much more liberated."

Morrissey further comments that, "In order to forgive her father, Julie needed to separate who he was from what he had done. She needed to separate him as a being from his terrible acts. To forgive means to give up one way of thinking for a higher way of thinking. We may not forgive the act perpetrated against us, but we can forgive the perpetrator, recognizing that behind every hurtful action lies a hurting person."

Reverend Morrissey cautions, "This does not mean that we do not need to protect ourselves or seek justice when someone behaves dangerously."

CHAPTER TWELVE

And Then
There Is Forgiveness

forgive, *verb*
1 a : *to give up resentment of or claim to requital for*
<forgive *an insult*>
b : *to grant relief from payment of* <forgive *a debt*>
2 : *to cease to feel resentment against (an offender) :*
PARDON <forgive *one's enemies*>
—Merriam-Webster's Dictionary*

Simply put, when we forgive, we "let go." Forgiveness does not mean to "excuse" offensive behavior. Forgiveness does not mean to "let go" of our safety. Forgiveness means to "let go" of resentment and find peace.

A very private friend of mine, a man in his late sixties, confided in me the torment he suffered as a child at the hands of his father. A deeply spiritual man, he admits, "I say a prayer for my father every morning, but try as I might; I am unable to forgive the 'son of a bitch.'"

Another friend of mine named Ann, told me a story about her father. Apparently his mother had abandoned

*By permission. From Merriam-Webster's Online Dictionary © 2003, www.Merriam-Webster.com by Merriam-Webster, Incorporated.

him at the age of five. Ann said, "My father died when he was seventy-seven, still unable to forgive his mother."

I am amazed at the number of elderly who still recount painful memories of their childhood abuse. I find battered souls everywhere bearing deep scars of physical and emotional trauma. Countless numbers of people carry broken children inside along with the legacy of hurt that lives in their hearts and crowds their souls.

For years, I have been frustrated with so many stories I either heard on the news and on talk shows, or read about which were all about abuse and forgiveness. So often, I hear the words: "You HAVE to forgive," followed by a narrative from one extreme to another. First one hears how bad their life of abuse was, which is immediately negated by how wonderful life is since the injured party has forgiven her abuser. However, most often these individuals neglect to explain the process in between. In one fashion or another, each survivor created a foundation of healing to build upon before they forgave. I have spoken with several people who have said, "How dare they tell me I HAVE to forgive. They don't know what I've been through! How can I just forgive?"

We need to help the abused through the healing process before we ask them to forgive. Most likely they can't and shouldn't forgive immediately. In fact, forgiveness almost certainly will take many years.

I have encountered several people who have forgiven their abusers in different ways.

- A man who, after a life of misery and his father's death, was finally able to confront his past, hold his dead father accountable and forgive.

- A woman who, after years of anger and creating continued chaos in her life, confronted her parents, who in turn accepted responsibility, made amends and offered restitution.

When an abusive parent is able to extend the gift of restoration and make amends, this is the greatest opportunity for healing. However, what if your parent is unwilling or unable to make amends? What if your parent is still living and continues to hurt you?

It took me years of searching for the answers to these questions before I learned how to receive the support and validation necessary to forgive a living parent unwilling to participate in the healing process.

I think it is easy to become impatient with forgiveness because healing takes an exceptionally long time. After I spent years receiving the validation I needed, I expressed my anger and grief and then I found myself starting all over again; each time at a deeper level.

This can feel like you are not making any progress; however, in retrospect I can see that each layer of recovery was dependant on my prior healing experiences.

At first, I simply acknowledged and understood how I was abused. Once I worked through this level of healing and lived with it for a while, I discovered numerous ways my abuse damaged me and I had to go through the validation, anger and mourning process all over again. I repeated these healing steps when I discovered how my abuse affected my adult relationships. Then again, when I realized I needed to heal my relationships and myself by replacing old unhealthy internal messages, feelings and responses, with new healthy internal messages, feelings and responses.

Many books are written on the subject of abuse, although few of them present the problems of physical and emotional violence and consequently the struggle to heal and forgive. Some books on the market portray forgiveness as a personal choice and therefore intentionally avoid the question of whether or not to forgive. Much of the material available concerning abuse adheres to the notion that forgiveness is not necessary or that parents must *earn* forgiveness. Other works offer the belief that forgiveness is essential, yet do not present the steps required to achieve forgiveness. Still other publications advocate for forgiveness but present only a partial depiction of the process.

Unable to find a comprehensive compendium of forgiveness with respect to abuse, I developed an illustration of the forgiveness process. I combined my personal experiences along with the various partial aspects of forgiveness I discovered in multiple works.

I went to the closet to retrieve my abandoned manuscript. I worked diligently to rewrite and revise my new title, *Heal and Forgive: Forgiveness in the Face of Abuse.*

* * * * *

Forgiveness begins with healing. When we are wounded, it is hard to recognize anything other than our pain. Sometimes it is necessary to set aside the notion of forgiveness, at least temporarily. This allows us the opportunity to focus on self-preservation, healing, and the re-evaluation of our relationship with the offender.

I stumbled onto healing quite by accident. After years of misery and burying my pain in order to pardon my mother, I abandoned my quest to forgive and took a risk. The day came when I reached the end of my endurance. I disobeyed my family, walked away from Mom, from years of abuse and told my story. That is how I happened on the first step to healing—validate your pain. This may sound obvious; however, many of us just don't see it.

VALIDATION

Validate your experience with friends, support groups, a competent therapist, or a combination of all three. For me, each time someone validated my experience, I became stronger and clearer about what happened to me and the effect that it had on my life. I also found great comfort and validation in reading stories that closely paralleled what I had survived.

For most survivors, abuse is our only reality. We don't know what it's like to live in a healthy family.

Even if we are already aware of our childhood abuse, we often live in denial about the effect the abuse has had on us. It is necessary to have another party bear witness to our trauma. This allows us the opportunity to admit to ourselves the ways in which we were damaged by our abuse. Support and validation offered from others, dissolves our isolation and gives us the necessary strength to journey forward to the life we deserve. Once our stories are heard, the door opens to recognizing our anger.

ANGER

Forgive and forget. Anger corrodes. Only through forgiveness can you heal. These often-heard statements usually instill within us a sense of urgency that implies we must forgive immediately. Yet, if forgiveness is hastened or forced, it usually doesn't last.

Steven Mosley, author of *Secrets of the Mustard Seed: Ten Life Changing Promises from the New Testament* devotes a chapter to forgiveness in which he ponders the question "How did Jesus forgive from the cross?" Mosley answers his inquiry this way:

> Jesus did something very important before he went to the cross. It's something we often overlook. He expressed anger. You find it laid out very vividly in Matthew 23, where he protests against whitewashed sepulchers full of greed and self-indulgence, blind guides leading the blind, and a brood of vipers shedding the blood of prophets. He expressed how outraged he was by the hypocrisy of those so desperately trying to kill him. He wanted to free people from their oppressive religiosity.

Mosley goes on to express the following selected thoughts:

- Expressing anger is one of the prerequisites of forgiving permanently. So we need to express our feelings instead of discounting them: *That was wrong. That really hurt me.*
- If we just ignore the hurt and try to smile our way through forgiveness, the pain will just come out in other ways.
- To forgive without expressing anger or disappointment is to forgive from a position of weakness.
- Forgiving from weakness only invites more hurt. It never quite catches up with the pain.

Laura Davis, author of *Allies in Healing: When the Person You Love Was Sexually Abused as a Child,* speaks of anger this way:

> Anger is the backbone of healing. Most survivors have been angry for years. Either they've turned it in on themselves or lashed out at others and become abusive themselves. As a survivor heals, she learns to direct her anger clearly and squarely at the abuser and the people who failed to protect her. The survivor needs to find safe, empowering ways to express her anger and let it out.

Expressing anger was a difficult lesson for me. From my earliest memories, the consequences of expressing anger were so detrimental that the suppression of my rage ate away at my soul—robbing me of the ability to feel anything else. It wasn't until I moved outside my family circle and found safe environments in therapy and with trusted friends that I was able to express my anger at my mother and brothers. Once others validated the horrors of my experiences, I was free to discharge my anger.

Finding the "safe" and "empowering" ways to express the anger that Laura Davis speaks of is not always easy. Yet, it is very important not to allow your anger to fester.

Once, while I was working through a particularly difficult incident, I found that my prior methods of anger release did nothing to diminish my rage.

I didn't know what to do. First, I thought about the list of exercises that I found in books and had used before:

- Write an angry letter to the person and burn it.

- Pound on my bed with my racquetball racket.
- Drive with my windows rolled up and scream at the top of my lungs.
- Break a whole set of old dishes.

None of these exercises was sufficient this time.

Finally, I enlisted the aid of a good friend. He suggested that since Mother's Day was approaching, we could make some "Mother's Day" cards. He brought some construction paper and crayons over to my house along with a multitude of ideas for making "Mother's Day" cards that would not be sent to the not-so-good mother.

We laughed for hours as we made our cartoonishly violent cards.

The release I felt when we were done was overwhelming.

GRIEF

Grieving is a very healing part of the process. Ellen Bass and Laura Davis stated it well in *The Courage to Heal: A Guide for Woman Survivors of Child Sexual Abuse*:

> **Grieving and Mourning.** As children being abused, and later as adults struggling to survive, most survivors haven't felt their losses. Grieving is a way to honor your pain, let go, and move into the present.

Once I released my anger, the vast accumulation of suppressed sadness rose to the surface. Like many other victims of childhood abuse, I learned that my survival depended on being tough enough to handle anything. Although I was acutely aware of—and compassionate to—the pain of other people, I was blind to my own suffering. Long into adulthood, I "powered" through every situation just to survive. I never learned how to process my own pain. Undoing a lifelong mechanism is a very difficult undertaking. In order to grieve—I needed to "unlearn" the way I learned to ignore my agony. Then I needed to re-learn a healthy method of expressing my sadness. It was very important for me to learn to cry for myself and to share those tears with others.

Each time I thought I had finished mourning, another wave of heartbreaking losses emerged. However, as I peeled away each layer of pain, I grew increasingly stronger.

PROTECTION

An important and often overlooked aspect to healing is that of protecting ourselves. In order to heal we must be free from the anxiety of re-injury. Depending on the type and severity of the offense, this could range anywhere from re-evaluating a relationship, to deciding not to see someone, or even criminal prosecution. In order to let go of the hurt, we must have assurances that the offender will harm neither ourselves nor anyone else. Most victims need to see some form of justice in order to let go.

The Reverend Dr. Marie M. Fortune, in *Abuse and Religion: When Praying Isn't Enough*, states, "Forgiveness before justice is 'cheap grace' and cannot contribute to authentic healing and restoration to wholeness for the victim or the offender."

Fortune, along with Richard Lord, author of *Do I Have to Forgive?*, agrees that remorse, repentance, and restitution are necessary prerequisites of forgiveness. However, Fortune delves further when she acknowledges, "Each step is dependent on the willingness of the offender to participate in the healing process, but often the offender is unwilling or unavailable."

Dr. Fortune goes on to examine the possibility of forgiveness in the absence of the participation from the wrongdoer, "Justice, forgiveness, and healing for the victim cannot be dependent on the offender. These steps then become the responsibility of the wider community. The church, the legal system, and family friends can also make justice for victims." She goes on to describe the elements of justice, including acknowledgment of the harm done to the victim, breaking the silence, hearing the whole story, and protecting the vulnerable.

Fortune further offers this advice to the community:

- Thus, when an offender is not remorseful or repentant, the survivor needs justice from other sources. Victims need to have their experience acknowledged by others within some wider context.
- Waiting patiently with victims until they are ready to forgive may be the most charitable and compassionate act the church can offer. In these ways, we take seriously the power of forgiveness to bring people to healing.

Just as Dr. Fortune's work reveals, my family was unwilling to participate in the healing process. I was fortunate enough to find people willing to help "make justice" by acknowledging my experiences and standing by me through the healing process.

Protecting myself required taking a huge risk. It was essential that I do the very thing that always got me in so much trouble—I needed to talk about the abuse. It is worth repeating that sharing was absolutely terrifying. However, much to my relief, people listened, they heard and they understood. I literally felt lighter. The "monster" I carried didn't feel quite so heavy.

In order to protect myself, I needed the support of others. I never would have been able to forgive my mother if I still had a relationship with her. As long as she continued to hurt me—I would not be able to heal and ultimately forgive.

CONCLUSION

It has been more than twelve years since I have seen my family. Like so many other people, forgiveness hasn't come easily for me. It has been a difficult journey of detours, wrong turns and dead ends!

Pressuring the victim of violence to forgive too soon places an additional burden on the individual that can slow down or damage recovery. Previous steps are required in order to forgive.

- Begin a journey of self-preservation.
- Validate and acknowledge your injuries.
- Express anger appropriately.
- Mourn your losses.
- Protect yourself and others.
- And then there is forgiveness.

Forgiveness does not happen all at once; for me, it happened slowly over many years. Even now that I finally feel forgiving, new hurts associated with my family occasionally crop up that I need to forgive.

Forgiveness is not an event of immediacy. It's not a bolt of light that brightens the soul and burns the pain to ashes. Forgiveness is a process that is transformational. When it was all said and done, the final process was an act of love for me—love of myself and love of my mother.

How ironic that it was the act of not forgiving that finally freed me to forgive.

Notes

CHAPTER FIVE

Bloomfield, Harold H. *Making Peace With Your Parents*. (New York: Random House, 1983), p. 18.

Vachss, Andrew. "You Carry the Cure in Your Own Heart." (New York: *Parade* Magazine, August 28, 1994), pp. 4-6. On-line at www.vachss.com. Reprinted with permission from PARADE, copyright © 1994.

CHAPTER SEVEN

Miller, Alice. Translated by Worrall, Simon. *Breaking Down the Wall of Silence: The Liberating Experience of Facing Painful Truth*. (New York: EP Dutton, 1991), pp. 131, 134.

Forward, Susan. *Toxic Parents: Overcoming Their Hurtful Legacy and Reclaiming Your Life*. (New York: Bantam Books, 1989), pp. 177-179.

CHAPTER EIGHT

Engels, Beverly. *Divorcing a Parent: Free Yourself from the Past and Live the Life You've Always Wanted*. (New York: Ballantine, 1991), pp. 9-10, 101-102.

Lord, Richard. *Do I Have to Forgive?* Copyright 1991 *Christian Century*. Reprinted with permission from the October 9, 1991, issue of the *Christian Century*. P. 902.

CHAPTER NINE

Engels, Beverly. *Divorcing a Parent: Free Yourself from the Past and Live the Life You've Always Wanted.* (New York: Ballantine, 1991), pp. 106-107.

CHAPTER TEN

Edelman, Hope. *Motherless Daughters: The Legacy of Loss.* (Delta, 1995), p.61.

CHAPTER ELEVEN

Miller, Alice. Translated by Worrall, Simon. *Breaking Down the Wall of Silence: The Liberating Experience of Facing Painful Truth.* (New York: EP Dutton, 1991), p. 134.

Morrissey, Mary Manin. *Building Your Field of Dreams.* (New York: Bantam Books, 1996), pp. 140-143. Copyright © 1996 by Mary Manin Morrissey. Used by permission of Bantam Books, a division of Random House, Inc.

CHAPTER TWELVE

Merriam - Webster's Dictionary. Unabridged online - http://www.m-w.com/cgi-bin/dictionary

Mosley, Steven. *Secrets of the Mustard Seed: Ten Life Changing Promises from the New Testament.* (Colorado Springs: NavPress, 2002), pp. 41-42. Used by permission of NavPress - www.navpress.com. All rights reserved.

Davis, Laura. *Allies in Healing: When the Person You Love was Sexually Abused as a Child.* (New York: HarperCollins Publishers, 1991), p. 34.

Bass, Ellen and Davis, Laura. *The Courage to Heal: A Guide for Woman Survivors of Child Sexual Abuse.* (New York: HarperCollins Publishers, 1994), p. 65.

Horton, Anne L. and Williamson, Judith A., edited by. *Abuse and Religion: When Praying Isn't Enough.* (Lexington, MA: Lexington Books, D.C. Heath and Company, 1988). Reprinted with permission from Lexington Books as it appears in:

Fortune, Marie M. *Violence in the Family – A Workshop Curriculum for Clergy and Other Helpers.* (Cleveland: Pilgrim Press, 1991), pp. 174-178.

About
Nancy Richards

Nancy Richards is an adult survivor of childhood abuse. She is the single parent of two thriving, adult daughters. Richards is a successful business woman, as vice president and general manager of a large wholesale food processing company in Seattle. She is a member of The International Women's Writing Guild. She makes her home in one of the city's suburbs.